Learning DHTMLX Suite UI

Create your first single-page JavaScript application using multiple DHTMLX components and a touch of HTML5

Eli Geske

PUBLISHING

BIRMINGHAM - MUMBAI

Learning DHTMLX Suite UI

First published: October 2013

Production Reference: 1221013

Published by Packt Publishing Ltd.
Livery Place
35 Livery Street
Birmingham B3 2PB, UK.

ISBN 978-1-84969-933-4

www.packtpub.com

Cover Image by Eli Geske (ejgeske@yahoo.com)

Credits

Author
Eli Geske

Reviewers
Asen Bozhilov

Ali Farhadi

Ed Wildgoose

Acquisition Editor
Kartikey Pandey

Julian Ursell

Commissioning Editor
Govindan K

Technical Editors
Dipika Gaonkar

Mrunmayee Patil

Project Coordinator
Amey Sawant

Proofreader
Lauren Harkins

Indexer
Hemangini Bari

Graphics
Ronak Dhruv

Production Coordinator
Kyle Albuquerque

Cover Work
Kyle Albuquerque

About the Author

Eli Geske is an entrepreneurial graphics designer turned programmer. He has been involved in web applications from creating and enhancing online gaming communities, to building applications that improve company's efficiency. He has also invented products, put in for patents, and pushed them to market. His programming skills range from JavaScript, PHP, and C# which he uses in the medical industry, payment processing industry, and on custom order management sites. He also has a degree in computer science, focusing on networking and web server administration.

His knowledge of DHTMLX springs from his daily engagements in a current large scale medical application.

Some other of Eli's writings and public offerings can be viewed on his blog `www.eligeske.com` or on `eligeske.github.com`.

Throughout the past couple of years, my daily involvement with the DHTMLX components Suite has included working with a wonderful development team locally and abroad. These people have given me the ability to expand my knowledge and learn new things. I'd like to send out thanks to Igor Lopez, Bruno Spinelli, Tengiz Tutisani, Jaya Uradhanda, Sergey Bilida, Dmitry Shumarov, and Sergio Reyes who are a part of that great team! I would also like to thank, Roberto and Victor Beraja, whose visions have stretched the DHTMLX library to its limits on more than one occasion. Cheers!

About the Reviewers

Asen Bozhilov is web developer with years of experience in web technologies. Currently, he is working on XULRunner applications using JavaScript and XUL. He has a bachelor's degree in computer science. In his spare time, he likes to experiment with new technologies and programming languages. His interests are mostly in the computer sciences, but he also enjoys sport activities.

He has reviewed other JavaScript books, such as *Maintainable JavaScript*, *JavaScript Patterns*, and *JavaScript for PHP developers*.

Ali Farhadi is a senior web developer and system administrator living in Mashhad, Iran. He is passionate about working on open source technology and has contributed to the major PHP frameworks, CakePHP, and Lithium.

He is also one of the pioneers in the Persian node.js community and has contributed to the core project since 2009. He has also authored a few open source projects notably the HTML5Sortable jQuery plugin and SMPP module for node.js.

You can read more about him and his works at his website `http://farhadi.ir`.

Ed Wildgoose grew up in the time when a ZX81 was cutting edge and spent his formative years slaving away in the finance world, before deciding that the way ahead was to start slaving away for even longer hours and less money as his own boss. He enjoys learning about the art of IT for its own sake and has played with most common (and uncommon) programming languages and tools over the years (Did anyone else enjoy using Haskell in the early 90s?). He has developed projects on Mac, Windows, and Linux over past years, but most currently favors Linux for backend servers and Mac on the desktop.

He currently owns MailASail (`http://mailasail.com`), a boutique, which supplies services for users with satellite phones and roaming cellular devices. MailASail is a leading supplier of satellite hardware and airtime, but specialize in offering in-house solutions, which optimize TCP data over the expensive satellite links, that is, you can grab your iPhone and read your email from the middle of an ocean, desert, or glacier, for a very affordable cost! Their customers range from BBC nature documentary creators through to ocean rowers.

I would like to thank my wife Sue, and, my children, Katie and Luke, for putting up without their father while he spent far too long working.

www.PacktPub.com

Support files, eBooks, discount offers, and more

You might want to visit www.PacktPub.com for support files and downloads related to your book.

Did you know that Packt offers eBook versions of every book published, with PDF and ePub files available? You can upgrade to the eBook version at www.PacktPub.com, and as a print book customer, you are entitled to a discount on the eBook copy. Get in touch with us at service@packtpub.com for more details.

At www.PacktPub.com, you can also read a collection of free technical articles, sign up for a range of free newsletters and receive exclusive discounts and offers on Packt books and eBooks.

http://PacktLib.PacktPub.com

Do you need instant solutions to your IT questions? PacktLib is Packt's online digital book library. Here, you can access, read and search across Packt's entire library of books.

Why Subscribe?

- Fully searchable across every book published by Packt
- Copy and paste, print and bookmark content
- On demand and accessible via web browser

Free Access for Packt account holders

If you have an account with Packt at www.PacktPub.com, you can use this to access PacktLib today and view nine entirely free books. Simply use your login credentials for immediate access.

Table of Contents

Preface

The DHTMLX components library is fast, fun, and exciting! If you are looking to build a user friendly, highly interactive web application, then DHTMLX is one of the best choices in the market today.

DHTMLX provides great individual components from grids, charts, forms, layouts, toolbars, and more that can all be used together or individually. Each of the components has great online documentation with many samples.

When starting to use new tools for programming, there is always a learning curve on how to use the documentation and where to start. This book aims to speed up your knowledge and shorten that learning curve exponentially! Welcome to the wonderful world of client-side programming!

What this book covers

Chapter 1, User Management Web App, provides a more in-depth look into why we chose DHTMLX over other libraries and explains exactly what we will be building.

Chapter 2, Download, Setup, and Test, covers how to get going with the DHTMLX library and where to put the downloaded files. It also touches on Chrome's developer tools.

Chapter 3, Data Structures, Storage, and Callbacks, jumps into the application code and creating our storage and callback methods. It also gives a crash course in HTML5 and local storage.

Chapter 4, The DHTMLX Layout, shows how to create a layout and its different initializations and then attach one to the application.

Chapter 5, The DHTMLX Toolbar, is all about the toolbar and how to create, disable, and listen to when they are clicked.

Chapter 6, The DHTMLX Grid, goes in-depth into the grid component and its methods and events, and then coding a grid to the application.

Chapter 7, The DHTMLX Window, goes in-depth into creating a pop-up window with the window component.

Chapter 8, The DHTMLX Form and Calendar, covers the form component and its different validation types and items, including a calendar or date picker.

Chapter 9, The DHTMLX Chart, covers the chart component showing different chart types, adding multiple data series, and manipulating the look and feel.

Chapter 10, The Finish Line, goes over the entire application, and discusses some common troubleshooting and how to enhance the application further on your own.

What you need for this book

HTML, CSS, and JavaScript knowledge is assumed, as this book will be using these three fields. The goal of this book is to show us how DHMTLX's components work. Therefore, we will not be focusing on structure of code or advanced JavaScript objects and in-depth explanations.

JSON and HTML5 will be used for data storage locally, as to not involve the server-side database. If you are not an expert on any of these, don't fret. Throughout the book, if you have any issues or don't understand something, go do a little studying and come back. This will not be hard; I promise.

A web server is needed. Unlike normal HTML files with inline JavaScript, DHTMLX should be run on a web server. There are many web server options out there for you to install. If using Mac, there is a built-in web server, or, if using Windows, you can use options such as WAMP. These are both extremely easy to set up. It is not in the scope of this book to go into installation of these.

A code editor and web browser with development tools is needed. You will need some type of code editor and a web browser with developer tools to debug our JavaScript. Since you may either be using a Mac or Windows, let's use Notepad++ as our editor and Google Chrome for our web browser and tools. This will make it easier to follow. But if you are set in your tools already and comfortable with them, please use those instead.

Who this book is for

This book targets anyone looking to build good looking web apps quickly, easily, and cleanly, with minimal cross-browser compatibility maintenance. The code you will write will be simple and not too advanced. If you are an expert backend developer, you will find better and more efficient ways to implement the application. For those of you who are not advanced developers, the code is clean and efficient enough to run this application without any issues at all in a production environment.

Conventions

In this book, you will find a number of styles of text that distinguish between different kinds of information. Here are some examples of these styles, and an explanation of their meaning.

Code words in text are shown as follows: "The `getUser` method retrieves the user object in a string from our `localStorage` and parses the JSON string back into an object."

A block of code is set as follows:

```
getUser: function(id){
  var user = localStorage.getItem(id));
  return (user)?JSON.parse(user):false;
},
```

New terms and **important words** are shown in bold. Words that you see on the screen, in menus or dialog boxes for example, appear in the text like this: "After it closes, re-open with the toolbar's **add** button."

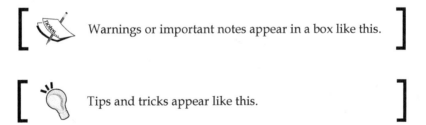

Warnings or important notes appear in a box like this.

Tips and tricks appear like this.

Reader feedback

Feedback from our readers is always welcome. Let us know what you think about this book—what you liked or may have disliked. Reader feedback is important for us to develop titles that you really get the most out of.

To send us general feedback, simply send an e-mail to feedback@packtpub.com, and mention the book title through the subject of your message.

If there is a topic that you have expertise in and you are interested in either writing or contributing to a book, see our author guide at www.packtpub.com/authors.

Customer support

Now that you are the proud owner of a Packt book, we have a number of things to help you to get the most from your purchase.

Downloading the example code

You can download the example code files for all Packt books you have purchased from your account at http://www.packtpub.com. If you purchased this book elsewhere, you can visit http://www.packtpub.com/support and register to have the files e-mailed directly to you.

Errata

Although we have taken every care to ensure the accuracy of our content, mistakes do happen. If you find a mistake in one of our books—maybe a mistake in the text or the code—we would be grateful if you would report this to us. By doing so, you can save other readers from frustration and help us improve subsequent versions of this book. If you find any errata, please report them by visiting http://www.packtpub.com/support, selecting your book, clicking on the **errata submission form** link, and entering the details of your errata. Once your errata are verified, your submission will be accepted and the errata will be uploaded to our website, or added to any list of existing errata, under the Errata section of that title.

Piracy

Piracy of copyrighted material on the Internet is an ongoing problem across all media. At Packt, we take the protection of our copyright and licenses very seriously. If you come across any illegal copies of our works, in any form, on the Internet, please provide us with the location address or website name immediately so that we can pursue a remedy.

Please contact us at copyright@packtpub.com with a link to the suspected pirated material.

We appreciate your help in protecting our authors and our ability to bring you valuable content.

Questions

You can contact us at questions@packtpub.com if you are having a problem with any aspect of the book, and we will do our best to address it.

1
User Management Web App

In this chapter, we will go over what DHTMLX is and the different ways in which we can use it. It is good to know that there are other options available and why DHTMLX stands out as a great choice for small-sized to full-sized web applications compared to others. We will also explain the application we will build, components that will be used, and what is needed to achieve this.

About DHTMLX

DHTMLX is a robust set of JavaScript components used for client-side, desktop-like web applications or websites. It also has server-side connection scripts to better help format the data structure to and from chosen types of server-side storage. Each of the DHTMLX's components can be used as individual features to your website or combined to create a full scale web application. All of these components work nicely together.

If you have been searching the Web for different components like grids or modal windows, you probably have seen some of the large variety of other options out there. There are jQuery-driven grids, custom JavaScript modal windows, and full scale libraries of components similar to DHTMLX.

DHTMLX and other component libraries

The major difference in the available JavaScript components is that most are small and contain only one or two different components. If you plan on just using a grid for a project, there are many good choices out there. Some of the better known smaller JavaScript component libraries for grids are jqGrid and SlickGrid.

Surprisingly, I have found that DHTMLX's grid has more options than even the single libraries specializing in grids. Also, one must be careful of choosing a standalone library, as the documentation and maturity can sometimes be an issue.

What about the more robust component libraries?

One of DHTMLX's comparable libraries is **Sencha Ext JS**. They both aim to give the developer the tools needed to build rich desktop-like applications in a web environment. They also provide both a free version as well as a paid version which includes support.

The major difference between these two component libraries is their documentation and coding structure. Sencha Ext JS has a very granular documentation that, when learned, is very beneficial. DHTMLX has a straight to the point list of available methods and events which are available for each component.

Today, more and more web designers want to make applications. These designers have a better understanding of a customer's needs and how to create a more user-friendly application. These designers may not have an in-depth understanding of programming and documentation. DHTMLX caters toward this very well.

The components

Let's get familiar with some of the components that DHTMLX has to offer and go over exactly what a component is.

A component in DHTMLX is a JavaScript object that is used to present and allow interaction of data to the end user in a clean and efficient manner. DHTMLX does all of the heavy lifting by creating the HTML in a presentable layout that is cross-browser friendly.

What is also important about a component is that they can be used together in a combination of components or separately in a block-level DOM element.

DHTMLX offers the following components:

- Grid
- Tree
- Tree Grid
- Layout
- Windows
- Toolbar
- DataView
- ColorPicker
- Editor

- Chart
- Menu
- Form
- Combo
- TabBar
- Calendar

 The DHTMLX team is hard at work adding new components frequently, so it is beneficial to check their website for a list of currently available components.

DHTMLX also provides an online skin builder and a Visual Designer tool. The skin builder allows for editing the CSS of a current skin or downloading one of the many existing skins. For our application, we will use the default "Blue Sky" skin.

The Visual Designer tool is a graphical user interface that allows a user to create code without having to actually write it. This is free, and is available on the DHTMLX website.

What will we be building?

Trumpets, please! We will be building a simple user management web application without a server-side database. Instead, we will be using HTML5's local storage. This will allow us to get going with DHTMLX quickly without being bound to a specific server-side language.

For the application, we will be using the Layout, Grid, Toolbar, Form, Chart, and Window components from the DHTMLX library. The app will provide the ability to add, delete, edit a user, and see charted data of those users in the system.

The following screenshot is what our final application will look like:

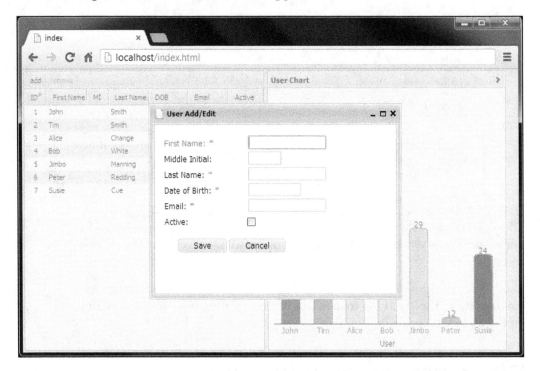

When you are finished with this book, you will have a good understanding of how to get the DHTMLX components to work together in a web application.

Summary

In this chapter, we covered what DHTMLX provides, which components are going to be utilized, and what our application will look like when completed. This brief introduction is enough to get us going.

In the next chapter, we will start the installation process by downloading and attaching the scripts in a local web server, then test that the library is installed correctly.

2
Download, Setup, and Test

In this chapter, we will go over downloading the DHTMLX library, creating the base files and directory structure, and including the library files. We will then write the configuration for the application and test the installation with Google Chrome developer tools.

Installing a web server

DHTMLX requires the application be used on a web server to allow all functionality to work. There are several preconfigured web server packages available for downloading on the Internet.

One of the options for Windows is WampServer. It is available at `http://www.wampserver.com`. For Mac users, one of the popular web server packages is MAMP. It is available at `http://www.mamp.info`.

Each of these websites provides instructions on using their packages.

Once you have a web server running, you must locate a directory accessible through the web server where you would like to create the application. The examples in this book will be using the root of an installed web server as the application directory and accessing the application at `http://localhost/`. The book will also refer to the `root` as the application directory.

Creating the application directory structure

Before downloading the DHTMLX components library, we need to create the application directory structure on our web server.

Locate the directory accessible on the web server where you will be hosting the application. This directory will be your application directory.

Now, create a new folder named js in the application directory. Inside the js folder, create a new folder named application and another named dhtmlx. Your directory structure should appear as shown in the following figure:

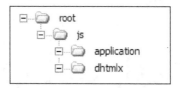

We will place all of the JavaScript files that we create for the application inside the application folder. The DHTMLX library code will be placed inside the dhtmlx folder.

Downloading the DHTMLX library

Now, we are going to download the DHTMLX library from their website and select which files will be used.

Open up your favorite web browser and navigate to www.dhtmlx.com. Here you will see a **Download** link in the menu. Click on the link. You should now see a page that looks like the following screenshot:

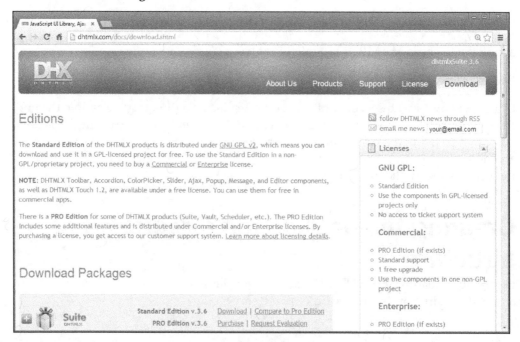

We want to download the entire library of components. DHTMLX calls this the **Suite**. Locate the **Download** link on the page for the **Standard Edition** of the Suite and click on the link. This will begin the download of a ZIP file. Download it to a location other than the application directory so that we can extract and choose which files we will use.

Open the extracted folder in your file manager to view its contents. You will see that it contains many folders, a license file, a readme file, an `index.html` file, and several more ZIP files.

 DHTMLX can be installed as individual components or as an entire suite.

The folders you see contain the individual components, which allow the individual use for each component.

The ZIP files contain the entire library of components in a compressed format in different skins.

The `index.html` file, when opened, provides the documentation for the downloaded version of DHTMLX. The DHTMLX documentation is broken down into two sections, documentation and samples, with details on each component. DHTMLX also provides the most up-to-date version of documentation on the website, but having a local copy is pretty handy when working offline, or if you have a slow network connection.

Next, we will extract the compressed version of the entire library to the application directory. Locate the ZIP file named `dhtmlx_std_full.zip`. This contains the actual DHTMLX files which we will use to build the application. Extract the contents of the `dhtmlx_std_full.zip` file to the `dhtmlx` folder in the `application` directory.

Once those have been extracted, we will start creating our application files.

Creating the application file app.js

The first application file is the `app.js` file. This will contain all of the JavaScript to create the components and interactions.

Let's start by creating the `app.js` file in the `js/application` directory.

Inside this file, add a `config` object at the top as shown in the following snippets:

```
var config = {
    imagePath: "js/dhtmlx/imgs/",
    iconPath: ""
}
```

This `config` object contains the global properties for the DHTMLX components. The `imagePath` property is the path where the images reside for the components styling. The second one which we left blank is the path where the icons will be stored. Icons can be used in several different components like the Modal Window header and the toolbar buttons.

Icons do not come with DHTMLX and have to be added from a free or purchased icons library.

The data storage file

The next file which we will create for the application is the `storage.js` file. This file will contain the mini data access layer that will speak to HTML5 localStorage. It will contain all of the CRUD methods for the users and displays.

Now, create a new JavaScript file in the `js/application` directory named `storage.js`. We will add code to this later.

Next, we will add an HTML file that will join the application code together.

Creating the index.html file

The application will be accessed through the `index.html` file located in the root of the application directory. We will set this up now.

In the root of the application directory, add a new file named `index.html`. This should be accessible from `http://localhost/index.html`.

Now, add the markup for an HTML5 document and include the external DHTMLX files:

```
<!DOCTYPE html>
<html lang="en">
   <head>
   <title>Users</title>
   <link href="js/dhtmlx/dhtmlx.css" type="text/css"
      rel="stylesheet" />
   <style>
      /* layout css */
      html, body { height: 100%; width: 100%; }
   </style>
<script src="js/dhtmlx/dhtmlx.js"></script>
<script src="js/application/storage.js"></script>
<script src="js/application/app.js"></script>
   </head>
   <body>
</body>
</html>
```

The dhtmlx.css and dhtmlx.js are the only DHTMLX library files necessary to include in the DHTMLX library for use. The storage.js and app.js are where the code for the user management application will be created.

Additional CSS was added that sets the html and body to a height and width of 100%. This will allow the DHTMLX layout component, added later, to stretch and grow when the browser window is resized. We will be adding more CSS here in later chapters.

The following screenshot displays how your final directory structure should appear:

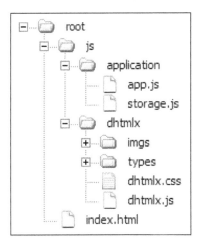

Testing the DHTMLX installation

We now have the necessary file structure and the index.html file created. This file includes the external DHTMLX CSS and JavaScript files for the application.

Next, we will talk about the Chrome developer tools and test if the DHTMLX library files were included correctly.

Open the Chrome web browser and navigate to http://localhost/ or http://localhost/index.html, loading the index.html file.

You should see a blank page displayed.

To make JavaScript development easy, Chrome provides the developer tools. This provides many useful tools for developing applications on the Web. The tool that we will focus on is the console. There are two ways to access the Chrome developer tools console window: through the Chrome menu or through keyboard shortcuts. Let's use the keyboard shortcuts approach. On Windows and Linux, the keyboard shortcut is *Ctrl + Shift + J*, and for Mac, it is *Cmd + Opt + J*. With the provided keyboard shortcuts, open the developer tools console window.

Inside the console window which you just opened, type the word dhtmlX. This will bring up the developer tools intellisense with all of the available properties and methods beginning with the word "dhtmlX". You should see something similar to the next screenshot:

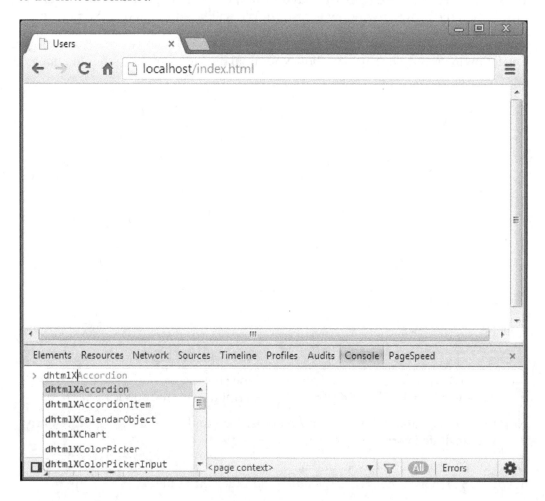

If the intellisense does not open or if you see errors in the console, check that you are including the files correctly.

Now, we will do a further test to check that the CSS is correct. For this we will add a DHTMLX layout object to the page.

Type the following line of code into the console and then press *Enter*:

```
new dhtmlXLayoutObject(document.body);
```

The page is now divided into three separate containers as shown in the following screenshot:

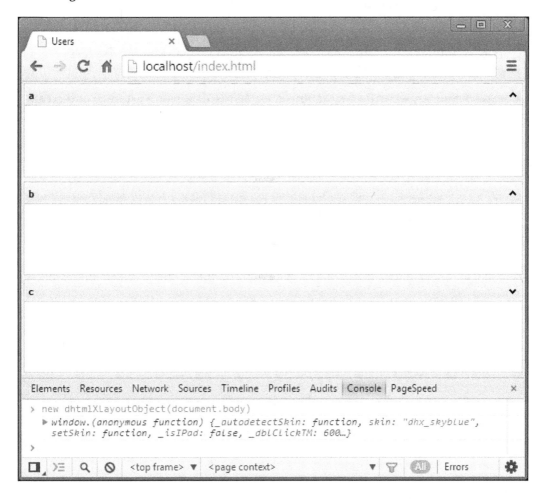

If you see only a gray screen, this means that you haven't added the height and width CSS styles to the HTML and body tag.

The three containers you see in the browser are the DHTMLX layout cells. These will be discussed in a later chapter. This simple test is enough to show that we have the files set up correctly. The installation and testing is now complete.

Summary

In this chapter, we covered downloading the DHTMLX Suite and the local documentation. We also created all of the necessary files to start the application, and explored using the Chrome developer tools. We touched on global configuration variables and what the storage file will be used for. You should be pretty comfortable for future chapters when asked to open one of these files or developer tools to add lines of code.

In the next chapter, we will start writing code that will access the storage and create the data structures for the components.

3
Data Structures, Storage, and Callbacks

In this chapter, we will explore how and where the user information will be stored, retrieved, and triggered for updating related data components. We will cover some cool features of HTML5 that will allow us to write the entire application on the client side. This will let us focus more on the user interface and the DHTMLX components, and alleviate maintaining a database and server-side code.

We will add a storage object to the storage.js file and add a callbacks object to the app.js file directly below our config object.

 DHTMLX has certain data structures for different components. For the grid and chart components, there will be separate calls to retrieve and structure the data.

localStorage

There has been a lot of buzz going around about HTML5 and its capabilities. We will cover one of them briefly.

Prior to HTML5 localStorage, the only option that client-side JavaScript had for storing persistent data across pages was utilizing cookies. Cookies are limited in size and do not remain only on the client side; they are sent to the server with each request. HTML5 localStorage considerably increases the storage limit and is strictly stored on the client side.

Some of the main reasons for utilizing localStorage are caching Ajax-served data, common form fields across pages, autocomplete results, or working offline. However, it is fairly new and implementation still varies slightly between browsers.

HTML5 localStorage allows the client side to store persistent data in key-value pairs across multiple browser windows restricted by the same-origin policy. The usage is simple. Here are the methods and properties we will be using to create the storage for our application:

```
localStorage.setItem(key,value) // sets item value
localStorage.getItem(key) // returns item value
localStorage.key(nth) // returns key of the enumeration
localStorage.clear() // clears all stored values
localStorage.length // returns number of items
```

These methods and properties are self-explanatory.

One important thing to know about localStorage is that the key and value parameters both are stored as DOMStrings. What this means to the application is that if an int is entered, it will be converted to a string version of that int. If you try to save an object, it will be returned as "[object type]", where type is the object type. So how do we store more complex objects into a localStorage item? We do so by using the JSON.stringify() method.

For the application, we will create JavaScript object literals and convert them to strings using the JSON.stringify() method prior to storing them. Then, upon retrieval, we will convert them back to an object using JSON.parse(). This is simple and allows us to save objects and retrieve object literals to localStorage.

Creating the storage object

Now, we will create the storage object. Find the storage.js file that we created, which should be empty. We will use the storage object to save and retrieve the application data.

 Please pay attention to trailing commas when adding methods to this JavaScript object. Every method should be followed by a comma. The last method is optional.

First, we will look at each individual method and what each one does. Then we will create the entire object.

The storage methods and properties

There are two properties we created in the storage object that are specific for helping it to operate.

lastStoredId

The first property is the `lastStoredId` property:

```
lastStoredId: localStorage.getItem("lastStoredId")? localStorage.
getItem("lastStoredId"):0,
```

This property retains the ID of the last entered item inside `localStorage`. Upon initial loading of the page, this property checks the `localStorage` item `lastStoredId` for a value. If it has one, that value is assigned to the `storage` object property `lastStoredId` property. If not, the `storage` object property `lastStoredId` property value defaults to 0.

This allows `localStorage` to act similarly to a database with incrementing primary keys. The storage object method will increment this property to create the user's ID when inserting a new user.

setDateFormat

The `setDateFormat` method is storage specific. It receives a JavaScript date object as its argument and converts it into readable string for storage. We will use this to format dates in other storage methods:

```
setDateFormat: function(date){
    var d = (date.getMonth() + 1);
    d += "-"+date.getDate();
    d += "-"+date.getFullYear();
    return d;
},
```

The user methods

The user methods will be used to create, update, remove, and retrieve user objects from `localStorage`.

The user model

The structure of our user model will be pulled directly from the values of the DHTMLX form we will be creating. Here is a preview of the data the form will contain:

```
{
    id: 1, // Int
    firstName: "John", // String
    middleInitial: "J", // String
    lastName: "Smith", // String
    dob: 1971-01-09T13:00:00.685Z, // Date
    email: "john@somedomain.com", // String
    active: 1 // Int (0,1)
}
```

createUser

The `createUser` method sets a new item and value into `localStorage`. This method takes a user object as an argument. We will also call one of the callbacks object methods, dataChanged. This will be covered when creating the callbacks object.

```
createUser: function(user){
    localStorage.setItem("lastStoredId", ++storage.lastStoredId);
    user.id = storage.lastStoredId;
    user.dob = storage.setDateFormat(user.dob);
    localStorage.setItem(user.id, JSON.stringify(user));
    callbacks.dataChanged();
},
```

The user parameter

This is the `user` object that will be retrieved from the DHTMLX form. Normally, one would create a user model to define the structure, but since our form will be driving all data changes for the user, it is safe to pull our data user model from the form.

When creating a user, there is no ID yet. That is where the `lastStoredId` comes in. We will set `lastStoredId` incrementally and then assign this as the user ID for storage. We then look at any form fields that a calendar is attached to. Since the calendar returns a JavaScript date object, it needs to be converted to a readable format. The **dob** field is the only field in the application form that has a calendar attached.

After the date field is formatted and the ID is created, the `user` object is saved to the `localStorage`. The ID is used for the `localStorage` key and the stringified version of the `user` object is used as the value.

getUser

The `getUser` method retrieves the `user` object as a string from `localStorage` and then parses the string into an object:

```
getUser: function(id){
    var user = localStorage.getItem(id));
    return (user)?JSON.parse(user):false;
},
```

updateUser

The `updateUser` method edits a `user` object by its ID:

```
updateUser: function(user){
    user.dob = storage.setDateFormat(user.dob);
```

```
    localStorage.setItem(user.id, JSON.stringify(user));
    callbacks.dataChanged();
},
```

removeUser

The `removeUser` method is the simplest method of them all. It removes a user object from `localStorage` by the user ID:

```
removeUser: function(id){
    localStorage.removeItem(id);
    callbacks.dataChanged();
},
```

The grid methods

The DHTMLX grid has a specific structure when loading data. It allows the use of several different data formats. This application will be using a JSON format. Be attentive to create the data structure as specified or the data will not load.

The grid JSON data structure

The next block of code is an example of how the data is structured. Studying this will help you understand why and how we created the grid methods:

```
data = {
    "rows": [
            {
                "id":1,
                "data":["col1","col2","col3","col4","etc"]
            },
            {
                "id":2,
                "data":["col1","col2","col3","col4","etc"]
            }
        ],
    "total_count": 2
}
```

The object we load into the grid has a rows array which contains an object for each of the user rows. The ID needs to be unique or the grid will not operate correctly.

Each individual object in the rows array has a property named `data`. This is an array of data for each column. The placement in the array corresponds to the column it will show in.

There is also another property called `total_count`. This is optional, but when using large data sets with any type of paging, DHTMLX utilizes this property. Additionally, this can be used to display the number of records in a status bar at the bottom of a grid.

gridRow

The `gridRow` method is exactly that. This will structure a `user` object into a formatted row item for use in the grid data:

```
gridRow: function(user){
    var data= [];
    data.push(user.id);
    data.push(user.firstName);
    data.push(user.middleInitial);
    data.push(user.lastName);
    data.push(user.dob);
    data.push(user.email);
    data.push((user.active)?"Yes":"No");
    return {
        "id": user.id,
        "data": data
    }
},
```

getUserGrid

The `getUserGrid` method will return the formatted object to be loaded into the DHTMLX grid. It loops through `localStorage` utilizing the `localStorage` key method, and checks to make sure we don't add our `lastStoredId` value to our grid. Next, the `gridRow` method formats the individual rows with the data retrieved from `localStorage`. Lastly, we structure the return object and add the `total_count` property with the value of rows length:

```
getUserGrid: function(){
    var rows = [];
    for(var i =0; i<localStorage.length; i++){
        var storageKey = localStorage.key(i);
        if(storageKey != "lastStoredId"){
            var row = localStorage.getItem(storageKey);
            row = JSON.parse(row);
            row = storage.gridRow(row);
            rows.push(row);
        }
```

```
        }
      return {
          "rows": rows,
          "total_count": rows.length
      }
    },
```

The chart methods

The DHTMLX chart has many different chart types to choose from. The one that will be used for the application is the bar chart. Similar to the grid, it has its own data structure. Here is a sample of what the chart data structure will look like:

```
[
    {"id":1,"age":35,"name":"FirstName1"},
    {"id":2,"age":29,"name":"FirstName2"}
]
```

Unlike the grid, which loads a JSON object, the bar chart will load an array. Each of the items in the array are objects with properties that will populate our chart values for each bar.

barChartItem

The `barChartItem` method is similar to the `gridRow` method. It returns formatted data from `localStorage` as an item to add to the overall chart data:

```
barChartItem: function(user){
    var getDateParts = function(date){
        return {
            d: date.getDate(),
            m: date.getMonth()+1,
            y: date.getFullYear()
        }
    }
    var date = getDateParts(new Date());
    var dob = getDateParts(new Date(user.dob));
    var age = date.y - dob.y;

    if(dob.m < date.m){
        age--;
    }
    if(dob.m == date.m && dob.d > date.d){
        age--;
    }

    return {
```

```
            "id" : user.id,
            "age" : age,
            "active": user.active,
            "name" : user.firstName
        }
    }
```

Here, we are using the `firstName`, `active`, and `dob` properties from the `user` object. Using the `dob` property, we calculate the age. Lastly, the item structure is created from these values and returned.

createUserBarChart

The `createUserBarChart` loops through `localStorage` retrieving the users then utilizing the `barChartItem` method to structure the item data:

```
getUserBarChart: function(){
    var items = [];
    for(var i =0; i<localStorage.length; i++){
        var storageKey = localStorage.key(i);
        if(storageKey != "lastStoredId"){
            var item = localStorage.getItem(storageKey);
            item = JSON.parse(item);
            item = storage.barChartItem(item);
            items.push(item);
        }
    }
    return items;
},
```

The storage object

Now that we have covered all of the methods for the storage object, have a look in the following code snippet to see the entire object. Please be aware that the code could be simplified, but it has been broken down for better understanding of changes that occur to the data in each method. Now, add the following code below to the `storage.js` file as shown:

```
var storage = {
    // Storage methods
    lastStoredId: localStorage.getItem("lastStoredId")?
      localStorage.getItem("lastStoredId"):0,
    setDateFormat: function(date){
        var d = (date.getMonth() + 1);
        d += "-"+date.getDate();
        d += "-"+date.getFullYear();
```

```
            return d;
    },
    // User Data
    createUser: function(user){
        localStorage.setItem("lastStoredId",
            ++storage.lastStoredId);
        user.id = storage.lastStoredId;
        user.dob = storage.setDateFormat(user.dob);
        localStorage.setItem(user.id, JSON.stringify(user));
        callbacks.dataChanged();
    },
    getUser: function(id){
        var user = localStorage.getItem(id);
        return (user)?JSON.parse(user):false;
    },
    updateUser: function(user){
        user.dob = storage.setDateFormat(user.dob);
        localStorage.setItem(user.id, JSON.stringify(user));
        callbacks.dataChanged();
    },
    removeUser: function(id){
        localStorage.removeItem(id);
        callbacks.dataChanged();
    },
    // Grid Data
    getUserGrid: function(){
        var rows = [];
        for(var i =0; i<localStorage.length; i++){
            var storageKey = localStorage.key(i);
            if(storageKey != "lastStoredId"){
                var row = localStorage.getItem(storageKey);
                row = JSON.parse(row);
                row = storage.gridRow(row);
                rows.push(row);
            }
        }
        return {
            "rows": rows,
            "total_count": rows.length
        }
    },
    gridRow: function(user){
        var data= [];
        data.push(user.id);
        data.push(user.firstName);
        data.push(user.middleInitial);
        data.push(user.lastName);
        data.push(user.dob);
        data.push(user.email);
        data.push((user.active)?"Yes":"No");
```

```
        return {
            "id": user.id,
            "data": data
        }
    },
    // Chart Data
    getUserBarChart: function(){
        var items = [];
        for(var i =0; i<localStorage.length; i++){
            var storageKey = localStorage.key(i);
            if(storageKey != "lastStoredId"){
                var item = localStorage.getItem(storageKey);
                item = JSON.parse(item);
                item = storage.barChartItem(item);
                items.push(item);
            }
        }
        return items;
    },
    barChartItem: function(user){
        var getDateParts = function(date){
            return {
                d: date.getDate(),
                m: date.getMonth()+1,
                y: date.getFullYear()
            }
        }
        var date = getDateParts(new Date());
        var dob = getDateParts(new Date(user.dob));
        var age = date.y - dob.y;

        if(dob.m < date.m){
            age--;
        }
        if(dob.m == date.m && dob.d > date.d){
            age--;
        }
        return {
            "id": user.id,
            "age": age,
            "name": user.firstName
        }
    }
}
```

The callbacks object

The next object we are creating is the `callbacks` object which will hold all of the methods that need to get updated or changed when another item is updated or changed.

Now, add the callbacks object code to the `app.js` file directly after the `config` object:

```
var callbacks = {
    // Toolbar
    addClick: function(){

    },
    removeClick: function(){

    },
    editClick: function(userId){

    },
    setToolbarItemStates: function(){

    },
    // Grid
    refreshGrid: function(){

    },
    // Chart
    refreshChart: function(){

    },
    // Popup
    showPopup: function(){

    },
    hidePopup: function(){

    },
    // User Data
    dataChanged: function(){

    }
}
```

This object is the glue that holds the data in sync across all of the application components. In each of the following chapters, we will be making additions to this object.

Summary

In this chapter, there was a lot covered. We created the `storage` object, which is the data access layer for the entire application. Then, we created the `callbacks` object and touched briefly on how this will be used.

All supporting application code is in place and we are ready to begin adding the DHTMLX components.

In the next chapter, we will learn about the DHTMLX layout component and attach one to the application.

4
The DHTMLX Layout

In this chapter, we will learn about the DHTMLX layout component covering the different initializations, events, methods, and settings. Then, we will create the main layout for the application.

All changes done in this chapter will occur inside the app.js file where we will add a creation method inside the page load event.

The DHTMLX layout

The DHTMLX layout is a powerful component that gives us the ability to create web interfaces. To put it in simple terms, it is a highly flexible container that we can attach many different components to. A layout can be used to split the page, or specified DOM container, into multiple horizontal and vertical panels to handle the placement of UI components. These individual panels are called cells. This is similar to dividing a page into containers with div or table elements. But unlike div and table elements, the DHTMLX cells can be resized, can grow and shrink with the page, and have multiple configurations.

The layout component is made up of itself, as the parent, and one or more child cells. DHTMLX provides predefined patterns when creating a layout. They range from dividing the page into columns, rows, or a combination of both. The predefined patterns are already available for use with the library code that was installed in the install chapter.

DHTMLX also provides more patterns that can be added via additional JavaScript files. The steps to do this are in the documentation for the layout component. For the application we are creating we will use the predefined pattern 2U. This pattern will divide the page into two columns.

The following figure shows the available predefined patterns along with their associated names:

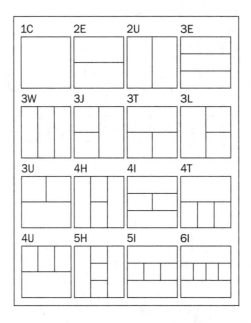

When developing an application you may find that one of the provided patterns does not fit your needs. DHTMLX does not currently provide a way to create a custom layout pattern. Until they do, the quickest way to customize a pattern is by building one with multiple layouts. This is done by attaching another layout to one or more child cells of a layout.

Some of the major benefits of the layout component are the built-in methods to attach other DHTMLX components. The layout and its cells give developers a means to easily create an iframe, HTML string, HTML object, and most of the DHTMLX suite components. When a layout is created to an HTML `body` tag all the components inside it will follow the resizing of the browser window, providing that the `body` tag has the CSS height and width of `100%`.

Check out the next screenshot of a 2U layout pattern to get an idea of how the layout and cells relate to each other:

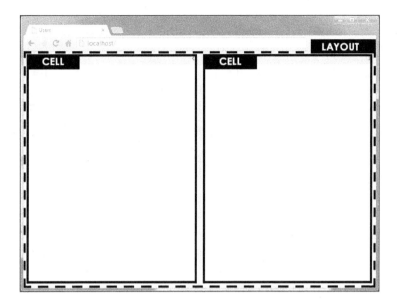

The methods and events

The DHTMLX layout is made up predominantly of two object types, one being the layout itself and secondly the cells which are its children. Why is this important to know? Some of the same methods can be called on either the layout object or the cell objects. But there are differences as you will see.

Now, open up the application in the Chrome browser with the developer tools console available. We will begin attaching layouts and learning the different methods and events which will help us better understand how the application is being developed.

Initialization

Initialization of a layout component can be done in two ways: by attaching a new layout object to an existing cell, or by attaching it to a DOM element on the page.

We will first attach a layout component to a DOM element and learn how to access the cells.

In your console type and run the following code:

```
new dhtmlXLayoutObject(document.body);
```

You should see a new three cell layout with a header of a, b, and c.

Let's clear that by refreshing the page; and then type and run the following code in the console:

```
new dhtmlXLayoutObject(document.body, "3E");
```

The same layout pattern was created because the second parameter for the layout constructor is the layout pattern. By default, DHTMLX sets the layout pattern 3E. You can choose from any of the predefined patterns we spoke of earlier.

Refresh the page once again so we can add a different layout and learn about accessing its cells. This time we need to assign a reference of the layout we create to a variable.

Type the following code in the console:

```
var myLayout = new dhtmlXLayoutObject(document.body, "2U");
```

As you can see we now have two cells. One shows "a" and other shows "b". When a layout is first created each child cell's header will have its cell ID as the text. This helps for quick identification. The cell's ID is how we will access that cell's object and its methods. Let's access one of the cells and attach a child layout component and save a reference to it.

Type and run the following code:

```
var myChildLayout = myLayout.cells("a").attachLayout("3E");
```

Attaching a layout component through this approach only uses one argument. Again this will default to the 3E pattern if an argument is not passed. Anytime a layout component is created the method used to create it will return the created layout object.

Each of the cells inside any created layout comes with a header bar that can expand or collapse until it is either removed or a child layout component is attached. Then the header for that cell is no longer visible.

Methods

Now, we will cover some of the methods available for the layout component and the individual cells.

Cell sizing

Of course with any design on an HTML page, we want to have control of widths and heights.

Refresh the page and create a layout that we can use to set the height and width. Type and run the following code:

```
var myLayout = new dhtmlXLayoutObject(document.body, "3T");
```

setHeight

Set the height of cell "a". Type and run the following code:

```
myLayout.cells("a").setHeight(55);
```

Now cell a has the height set to 55 pixels.

setWidth

Set the width of cell "b". Type and run the following code:

```
myLayout.cells("b").setWidth(70);
```

Now cell b has the width set to 70 pixels.

fixSize

You may have noticed when creating a layout that each cell is separated by a divider. This divider can be dragged to resize the cells in the page. This feature can be disabled by using the fixSize() method.

The fixSize() method takes the arguments of the x and y axis as Boolean or truthy and falsy values, stating whether or not each axis can be resized.

Type and run the following code:

```
myLayout.cells("b").fixSize(0,1);
```

Cell b and any cells sharing the x axis divider can no longer be sized vertically.

Type and run the following code:

```
myLayout.cells("b").fixSize(1,1);
```

Cell b and any cells sharing the y axis divider can no longer be sized horizontally.

Cell header

Each cell has a header that we can manipulate by collapsing, changing the text, hiding, or showing.

showHeader and hideHeader

The showHeader and hideHeader methods show and hide the cell header.

Type and run the following code:

```
myLayout.cells("c").hideHeader();
```

Then type in the given code and run the following:

```
myLayout.cells("c").showHeader();
```

setText

DHTMLX sets the header text of a cell to the cell ID by default. To change this text we use the setText method.

Type and run the following code:

```
myLayout.cells("a").setText("My Top Cell");
```

progressOn and progressOff

When building a JavaScript application with Ajax, it is important to provide an indicator during wait periods. This allows the person behind the keyboard to know that they are waiting for something to be returned and if necessary block some interface features from being used.

Both the layout object and cell object have the ability to show an indicator. The methods to do so are the progressOn() and progressOff() methods.

Now we will see what these look like with the layout we created.

Type and run the following code:

```
myLayout.progressOn();
```

The ability to access any interface functionality inside this layout is now blocked.

Now, turn off that progress indicator.

Type and run the following code:

```
myLayout.progressOff();
```

Try these methods on a cell object. There is a styling difference in the progress indicators for a layout object and cell object. These progress indicators can be easily styled with CSS.

Overview of methods

We covered the more commonly used methods for the DHTMLX layout and cell objects and the ones we will use in building the application. DHTMLX provides many advanced features you can explore like views, auto sizing, and docking/undocking.

Layout events

Events in JavaScript are very useful when creating applications. DHTMLX has provided many different events for each of the components. We will go over how to attach and detach one of the events to give us an idea of how we can utilize them.

The more common events for the layout object are `onResizeFinish`, `onExpand`, `onCollapse`, and `onDblClick`. Let's take a look at `onResizeFinish`.

We will use the same layout we created in previous sections to attach this event.

attachEvent and detachEvent

DHTMLX provides the `attachEvent` and `detachEvent` methods.

The first parameter when attaching an event is the name of the event you want to attach. The second is a handler method, which is the method that will fire when the event triggers.

Type and run the following code:

```
var myEventId = myLayout.attachEvent("onResizeFinish", function(){
    console.log("Layout Resized");
});
```

Now if you resize the browser window you will see a console entry stating **Layout Resized**.

In most cases the DHTMLX event will pass some parameters back to the handler method. Since this is just telling us the layout has been resized it passes nothing back.

To detach an event we use the returned event ID from the `attachEvent` method. For the event we just created, this event ID was assigned to the `myEventId` variable. Now, we will use this to detach that same event.

Type and run the following code:

```
myLayout.detachEvent(myEventId);
```

The console no longer logs the text from the event.

If you want to clear all of the events created on a certain layout object you could also use `myLayout.detachAllEvents()`, passing no arguments.

dhtmlxEvent

Similar to other JavaScript libraries, DHTMLX also has its own method to attach HTML DOM events to the HTML DOM elements. It takes three arguments; the first being the DOM element, the second being the HTML DOM event name without the "on" prefix, and lastly the handler. We will be using this to load each of the application parts on the page load:

```
dhtmlxEvent(window,"load", function(){
    // Code to be run on page load
});
```

All events in DHTMLX when added to the same event for the same object are added to an internal array that will be fired in the order it was added.

The application code

Now that we have covered how to use the DHTMLX's layout component, we are ready to create a layout for the application. Open the app.js file and get ready to start writing the code.

Create the layout

Enter the following code directly below the config object in the app.js file:

```
// Layout
var appLayout;
dhtmlxEvent(window, "load", function(){
    appLayout = new dhtmlXLayoutObject(document.body, "2U");
    appLayout.cells("a").hideHeader();
    appLayout.cells("b").setText("User Chart");
});
```

First, we defined the global variable `appLayout` that will allow us access to the layout in other methods of the application. Then we created the layout wrapped in a page load event. When the page loads the layout will be created.

After refreshing the page it will look like the following screenshot:

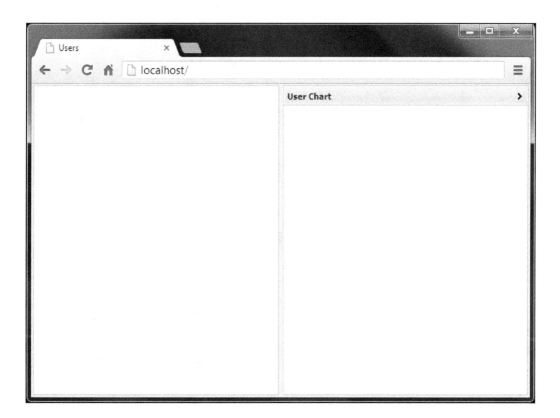

Summary

In this chapter, we went over the DHTMLX layout component and its commonly used methods and events. We then created the main layout for the application. Everything in the following chapters will be created in and around this layout.

In the next chapter, we will learn about the DHTMLX toolbar component and create one for the application.

5
The DHTMLX Toolbar

In this chapter, we will learn about the DHTMLX toolbar component and its different initializations, events, methods, and settings. Then we will add a toolbar to the application, giving it the ability to delete and add a user.

All changes made in this chapter will occur inside the app.js file.

The DHTMLX toolbar

The DHTMLX toolbar is a very handy component for applications or web pages. It allows us to quickly and easily create a robust series of buttons, dropdowns, and inputs.

When creating a DHTMLX toolbar, we have the freedom to place it inside a DOM element, a DHTMLX layout or a DHTMLX cell. But when attaching toolbars to the DHTMLX layout or cell, each are both limited to one. The following screenshots shows the differences of attaching a toolbar to a layout object and a cell object.

This screenshot shows an empty toolbar and what it looks like when one is attached to a layout object:

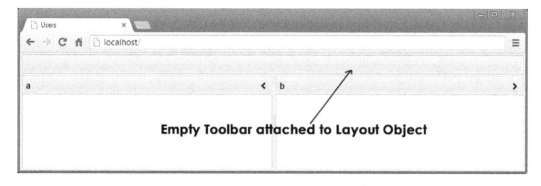

This screenshot shows a toolbar attached to a cell object:

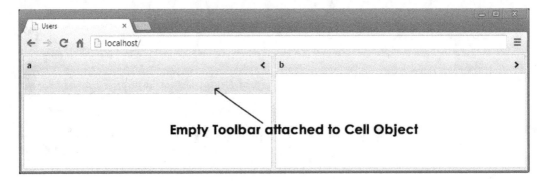

Empty Toolbar attached to Cell Object

The methods and events

Now open up the Chrome browser with the developer tools visible console, and we will begin to learn about the DTHMLX toolbar object. We will attach a toolbar, add toolbar items, and bind events.

Initialization choices

The DHTMLX toolbar can be initiated in two ways. The first way is by attaching it to a DOM element. The second way is by attaching it to an existing DHTMLX layout or cell.

Initialization on a DOM element

First we will attach a toolbar to a DOM element. For these exercises, we will be using the same web page as the application. To test attaching a toolbar to a DOM element, we must first clear the page and create an element inside the body tag. We will do this with JavaScript.

Type and run the following code line in the console:

```
document.body.innerHTML = "<div id='myToolbarCont'></div>";
```

We just cleared the contents of the body and replaced it with a div tag that has the id attribute of myToolbarCont.

Next initialize and attach a toolbar to that div.

Type and run the following code line in the developer tools console:

```
new dhtmlXToolbarObject("myToolbarCont");
```

The result will show an empty toolbar on the page.

Initialization on a layout object

In the previous chapter, we created a reference of the returned value from the createLayout method to the global variable named appLayout. We will use this to access the layout and its child cells for these next exercises.

First refresh the page to clear the previous exercise. Then type and run in the developer tools console:

```
appLayout.attachToolbar();
```

You will now see the toolbar attached to the overall layout, spanning across both cells.

Initialization on a cell object

Now let's add another toolbar, this time to one of the child cells.

Type and run the following code line in the developer tools console:

```
appLayout.cells("a").attachToolbar();
```

Now you should see an empty toolbar in the left cell of the layout.

DHTMLX does not currently allow more than one toolbar per container. But the same effect can be achieved by creating a child layout object inside a cell and attaching toolbars to each of those. We will try this now.

First refresh the page to reset.

Now we will create a child layout. Type and run the following code line in the console:

```
var childLayout = appLayout.cells("a").attachLayout("1C");
```

This adds a nested layout inside one of the cells.

With this additional layout object we can now start adding toolbars to each object.

Type and run the following code line in the console:

```
appLayout.cells("a").attachToolbar(); // 1st toolbar
childLayout.attachToolbar(); // 2nd toolbar
childLayout.cells("a").hideHeader(); // hide cell header
childLayout.cells("a").attachToolbar(); // 3rd toolbar
```

There are now three toolbars appearing one on top of the other.

Now that we know how to initialize a DHTMLX toolbar, we can start adding items.

Toolbar items

The DHTMLX toolbar has several different item types:

- Button
- Two-state button (Toggle)
- Button select (Select)
- Slider
- Input
- Text (Label)
- Separator
- Spacer

We will now go over each of them and see how they work.

First refresh the page to clear the previous exercise code.

Now we will add a new toolbar to cell a. We will use this toolbar to add the items for the next exercises.

Type and run the following code line in the console:

```
var myToolbar = appLayout.cells("a").attachToolbar();
```

 When adding items to the toolbar; if the items exceed the width of the cell, those items will not be visible. For this exercise, make sure you have enough cell width to show all items that will be added.

addButton

The addButton method adds a button to a toolbar. Buttons are a clickable item that can have text and an icon.

The parameters are the ID of the button, its position in the toolbar, the button text, an enabled icon (optional), and lastly a disabled icon (optional).

Type and run the following code line in the console:

```
myToolbar.addButton("myButtonId", 0, "My Button");
```

Now, there is a button added to the toolbar with the text of My Button.

addButtonTwoState

The addButtonTwoState method creates a toggle button, which keeps a Boolean state. This method has the same parameters as the addButton method. When this item is clicked, it fires the toolbar's onStateChange event.

Type and run the following code line in the console:

```
myToolbar.addButtonTwoState("myButton2StateId", 1, "2 State");
```

Now there is a new item on the toolbar with the text of **2 State**. When this new item is clicked, it will toggle between active and inactive.

getItemState

The getItemState method is used to retrieve the pressed state for the **two-state** button and returns a Boolean.

Type and run the following code line in the console:

```
myToolbar.getItemState("myButton2StateId");
```

This returns either true or false in the console.

addSeparator

The addSeparator method creates a vertical line to show a division between the toolbar items. The only parameters are ID and position.

Type and run the following code line in the console:

```
myToolbar.addSeparator("sepId", 2);
```

Now there is a separator line to the right of the **two-state** button.

addText

The `addText` method creates a text item. This is helpful when you need to create a label for another toolbar item.

Type and run the following code line in the console:

```
myToolbar.addText("myTextId", 3, "A Label: ");
```

There is a text item on the toolbar to the right of the separator.

addButtonSelect

The `addButtonSelect` method is a little more complicated than the previous items. This creates a select button similar to an HTML select element.

The parameters are the ID, position, text, JavaScript array of the options, an enabled icon (optional), a disabled icon (optional), and additional advanced parameters.

The following is an example for the JavaScript array of options. The parameters are ID, type, text, and icon (optional).

```
["myOptionId", "obj", "Option 1", "icon.gif"]
```

Now let's add a select button to the toolbar. Type and run in the console:

```
myToolbar.addButtonSelect("mySelectId", 4, "Select Me",[
    ["option1", "obj","Option 1"],
    ["option2", "obj","Option 2"]
]);
```

There is now a select button added to the toolbar. Clicking on the arrow will open the select button items. When an option is selected, the option gets highlighted. A selection is remembered the next time the select button is opened.

 There are additional parameters in the DTHMLX documentation for the `addButtonSelect` method that allow the created select button to behave more like an HTML select element.

getListOptionSelected

The `getListOptionSelected` method will return the ID of the currently selected item in the select button.

Type and run the following code line in the console:

```
myToolbar.getListOptionSelected("mySelectId");
```

In the console, the currently selected option ID is returned.

addSpacer

The `addSpacer` method divides the left side of the toolbar from the right. The items to the right of the item with the spacer will now will be aligned to the right in the toolbar.

The only parameter this takes is the ID of the toolbar item you would like to add the spacer to. We will add this to the first button with the ID of `myButtonId`.

Type and run the following code line in the console:

```
myToolbar.addSpacer("myButtonId");
```

Now all of items to the right of My Button are aligned to the right of the toolbar.

removeSpacer

The `removeSpacer` method removes a spacer from the toolbar. Type and run the following code line in the console:

```
myToolbar.removeSpacer("myButtonId");
```

The toolbar spacer is now removed and all items are aligned to the left.

addSlider

The `addSlider` method creates a slider item, which will hold the value for later retrieval either on an event or specific request. The parameters for this item are ID, position, length of slider in pixels as integer, minimum value, maximum value, current value, label left side, label right side, and tooltip (optional).

Type and run the following code line in the console:

```
myToolbar.addSlider("mySliderId", 5, 40, 1, 10, 4, "Low", "High");
```

addInput

The `addInput` method creates a form like input in the toolbar. Its parameters are ID, position, initial value, and width in pixels as `int`.

Type and run the following code line in the console:

```
myToolbar.addInput("myInputId",6,"Hi", 30);
```

We now have an input with a default value of `Hi`.

getValue

The `getValue` method returns the value of a slider or input toolbar item.

Type and run the following code line in the console:

```
myToolbar.getValue("myInputId");
```

You now see in the console, the initial value we set for the input. disableItem and enableItem.

The `disableItem` renders an item disabled and `enableItem` does the reverse.

Type and run the following code line in the console:

```
myToolbar.disableItem("myButtonId");
```

The button is now disabled and will not trigger any events.

Now enable the button. Type and run the following code line in the console:

```
myToolbar.enableItem("myButtonId");
```

hideItem and showItem

The `hideItem` hides the toolbar item and the `showItem` does the reverse.

Type and run the following code line in the console:

```
myToolbar.hideItem("myButtonId");
```

Type and run the following code line in the console:

```
myToolbar.showItem("myButtonId");
```

Hiding and showing toolbar items can be helpful when restricting permissions to features.

removeItem

The `removeItem` method removes an item from the toolbar. Type and run the following code line in the console:

```
myToolbar.removeItem("myInputId");
```

The input is now removed from the toolbar.

Toolbar events

Now that we have covered the different types of items and how to get their values, we will talk about the events that can be triggered. The toolbar events we will cover are `onClick`, `onStateChange`, `onValueChange`, and `onEnter`.

The parameters for these events are the event name and handler function.

When triggered, the event handler will provide an argument of the item ID which triggered the event.

onClick

The `onClick` event listens to any clicks on the toolbar's items.

Let's add this event to the toolbar. Type and run the following code line in the console:

```
myToolbar.attachEvent("onClick", function(itemId){
    console.log(itemId);
});
```

Now, click on the toolbar button item and see the item ID being logged in the console. Also note that the select button will act as a button when clicking left of the arrow.

onValueChange

The `onValueChange` event fires when the toolbar slider item value is changed.

onStateChange

The `onStateChange` event fires when the toolbar two-state button item state is changed.

onEnter

The `onEnter` event fires when the *Enter* key is pressed inside the toolbar input item.

The application code

We covered a lot of what DHTMLX has to offer in its toolbar component. This will get us going for the application code.

Open the `app.js` file and get ready to start writing code.

Creating the toolbar

Now we will create the toolbar for the application. We will use a JavaScript object literal to create the toolbar.

Enter the following code directly below where the layout is created in the `app.js` file:

```
// Toolbar
var appToolbar;
dhtmlxEvent(window, "load", function(){
    // create toolbar
    appToolbar = appLayout.cells("a").attachToolbar({
        items: [
            { type: "button", id: 1, text: "add" },
            { type: "separator", id: 2 },
            { type: "button", id: 3, text: "remove" },
            { type: "separator", id: 4 },
        ]
    });
    // attach toolbar events
    appToolbar.attachEvent("onClick", function(id){
        switch(id){
            case "1": callbacks.addClick(); break;
            case "3": callbacks.removeClick(); break;
            default: break;
        }
    });
});
```

We first defined the global `appToolbar` variable to allow access to the toolbar in other methods in the application. Then we initialized the toolbar and attached the `onClick` event.

Inside the event handler is a switch statement that will fire the method we need that corresponds to the toolbar item's ID.

Now refresh the page and see the newly created toolbar. The following screenshot shows how the application looks now:

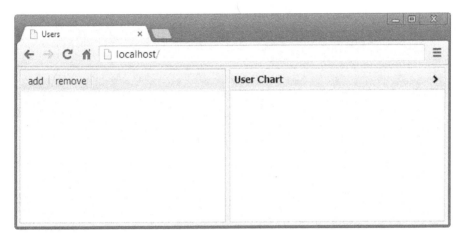

Summary

In this chapter, we went over the DHTMLX toolbar component and its items. We learned how to use its events and retrieve values. Then we added a toolbar to the application.

In the next chapter, we will learn about the DHTMLX grid component and add one to the application.

6
The DHTMLX Grid

In this chapter, we will learn about the DHTMLX grid component covering the different initializations, events, methods, and settings. We will then add a grid to the application that will control the user data.

All changes done in this chapter will occur inside the app.js file.

In this chapter, we will start adding code to the callbacks object and use the storage object for the first time.

The DHTMLX grid

The DHTMLX grid component is one of the more widely used components of the library. It has a vast amount of settings and abilities that are so robust we could probably write an entire book on them. But since we have an application to build, we will touch on some of the main methods and get into utilizing it.

Some of the cool features that the grid supports is filtering, spanning rows and columns, multiple headers, dynamic scroll loading, paging, inline editing, cookie state, dragging/ordering columns, images, multi-selection, and events.

By the end of this chapter, we will have a functional grid where we will control the editing, viewing, adding, and removing of users.

The grid methods and events

When creating a DHTMLX grid, we first create the object; second we add all the settings and then call a method to initialize it. After the grid is initialized data can then be added.

The order of steps to create a grid is as follows:

1. Create the grid object
2. Apply settings
3. Initialize
4. Add data

Now we will go over initializing a grid.

Initialization choices

We can initialize a DHTMLX grid in two ways, similar to the other DHTMLX objects. The first way is to attach it to a DOM element and the second way is to attach it to an existing DHTMLX layout cell or layout.

 A grid can be constructed by either passing in a JavaScript object with all the settings or built through individual methods.

Initialization on a DOM element

Let's attach the grid to a DOM element. First we must clear the page and add a div element using JavaScript.

Type and run the following code line in the developer tools console:

```
document.body.innerHTML = "<div id='myGridCont'></div>";
```

We just cleared all of the body tags content and replaced it with a div tag having the id attribute value of myGridCont.

Now, create a grid object to the div tag, add some settings and initialize it.

Type and run the following code in the developer tools console:

```
var myGrid = new dhtmlXGridObject("myGridCont");
myGrid.setImagePath(config.imagePath);
myGrid.setHeader(["Column1", "Column2", "Column3"]);
myGrid.init();
```

You should see the page with showing just the grid header with three columns.

Next, we will create a grid on an existing cell object.

Initialization on a cell object

Refresh the page and add a grid to the `appLayout` cell.

Type and run the following code in the developer tools console:

```
var myGrid = appLayout.cells("a").attachGrid();
myGrid.setImagePath(config.imagePath);
myGrid.setHeader(["Column1","Column2","Column3"]);
myGrid.init();
```

You will now see the grid columns just below the toolbar.

Grid methods

Now let's go over some available grid methods. Then we can add rows and call events on this grid.

For these exercises we will be using the global `appLayout` variable.

Refresh the page.

attachGrid

We will begin by creating a grid to a cell.

The `attachGrid` method creates and attaches a grid object to a cell. This is the first step in creating a grid.

Type and run the following code line in the console:

```
var myGrid = appLayout.cells("a").attachGrid();
```

setImagePath

The `setImagePath` method allows the grid to know where we have the images placed for referencing in the design. We have the application image path set in the `config` object.

Type and run the following code line in the console:

```
myGrid.setImagePath(config.imagePath);
```

setHeader

The `setHeader` method sets the column headers and determines how many headers we will have. The argument is a JavaScript array.

Type and run the following code line in the console:

```
myGrid.setHeader(["Column1", "Column2", "Column3"]);
```

setInitWidths

The `setinitWidths` method will set the initial widths of each of the columns. The asterisk mark (*) is used to set the width automatically.

Type and run the following code line in the console:

```
myGrid.setInitWidths("125,95,*");
```

setColAlign

The `setColAlign` method allows us to align the column's content position.

Type and run the following code line in the console:

```
myGrid.setColAlign("right,center,left");
```

init

Up until this point, we haven't seen much going on. It was all happening behind the scenes. To see these changes the grid must be initialized.

Type and run the following code line in the console:

```
myGrid.init();
```

Now you see the columns that we provided.

addRow

Now that we have a grid created let's add a couple rows and start interacting.

The `addRow` method adds a row to the grid. The parameters are ID and columns.

Type and run the following code in the console:

```
myGrid.addRow(1,["test1","test2","test3"]);
myGrid.addRow(2,["test1","test2","test3"]);
```

We just created two rows inside the grid.

setColTypes

The setColTypes method sets what types of data a column will contain.

The available type options are:

- ro (readonly)
- ed (editor)
- txt (textarea)
- ch (checkbox)
- ra (radio button)
- co (combobox)

Currently, the grid allows for inline editing if you were to double-click on grid cell. We do not want this for the application. So, we will set the column types to read-only.

Type and run the following code in the console:

```
myGrid.setColTypes("ro,ro,ro");
```

Now the cells are no longer editable inside the grid.

getSelectedRowId

The getSelectedRowId method returns the ID of the selected row. If there is nothing selected it will return null.

Type and run the following code line in the console:

```
myGrid.getSelectedRowId();
```

clearSelection

The clearSelection method clears all selections in the grid.

Type and run the following code line in the console:

```
myGrid.clearSelection();
```

Now any previous selections are cleared.

clearAll

The `clearAll` method removes all the grid rows. Prior to adding more data to the grid we first must clear it. If not we will have duplicated data.

Type and run the following code line in the console:

```
myGrid.clearAll();
```

Now the grid is empty.

parse

The `parse` method allows the loading of data to a grid in the format of an XML string, CSV string, XML island, XML object, JSON object, and JavaScript array. We will use the `parse` method with a JSON object while creating a grid for the application.

Here is what the `parse` method syntax looks like (do not run this in console):

```
myGrid.parse(data, "json");
```

Grid events

The DHTMLX grid component has a vast amount of events. You can view them in their entirety in the documentation. We will cover the `onRowDblClicked` and `onRowSelect` events.

onRowDblClicked

The `onRowDblClicked` event is triggered when a grid row is double-clicked. The handler receives the argument of the row ID that was double-clicked. Type and run the following code in console:

```
myGrid.attachEvent("onRowDblClicked", function(rowId){
    console.log(rowId);
});
```

Double-click one of the rows and the console will log the ID of that row.

onRowSelect

The onRowSelect event will trigger upon selection of a row.

Type and run the following code in console:

```
myGrid.attachEvent("onRowSelect", function(rowId){
    console.log(rowId);
});
```

Now, when you select a row the console will log the ID of that row. This can be perceived as a single click.

The application code

Now, we are going to create the user grid for the application. First, we will make the method that creates the grid and events. Then, we will add logic to the callbacks object and test the storage object code.

Create the grid

Open the app.js file and add the following code at the end:

```
// Grid
var appGrid;
dhtmlxEvent(window, "load", function(){
    // create grid
    appGrid = appLayout.cells("a").attachGrid();
    appGrid.setHeader(["ID","First Name","MI",
        "Last Name","DOB","Email","Active"]);
    appGrid.setColTypes("ro,ro,ro,ro,ro,ro,ro");
    appGrid.setInitWidths("35,*,35,*,75,*,55");
    appGrid.setColAlign("center,left,center,left,center,left,center");
    appGrid.setImagePath(config.imagePath);
    appGrid.init();

    // attach grid events
    appGrid.attachEvent("onRowDblClicked", function(rowId){
        callbacks.editClick(rowId);
    });
    appGrid.attachEvent("onRowSelect", function(){
        callbacks.setToolbarItemStates();
    });
    // reset grid and load it with data
    callbacks.refreshGrid();
});
```

First, we created the global `appGrid` variable that holds the reference to the grid. Next the grid is created and settings are applied. We then attached the events that will be used and added the method that will refresh the grid data.

Now, we will add the code to the `callbacks` object to handle the grid events and the refreshing of the grid data.

callbacks.setToolbarItemStates

Inside the `app.js` file locate the `callbacks` method `setToolbarItemStates`.

This method will disable and enable the **remove** button on the toolbar. Add the following code to the `setToolbarItemStates` method as shown:

```
setToolbarItemStates: function(){
    if(appGrid.getSelectedRowId()){
        appToolbar.enableItem(3);
    }else{
        appToolbar.disableItem(3);
    }
},
```

When this method is used it will check the grid for a selection and enable or disable the **remove** button.

callbacks.removeClick

The `removeClick` method will fire when the **remove** button is clicked. When this happens we will remove the selected user from the `localStorage` with the `storage` method `removeUser`.

Add the following code to the `callbacks` object `removeClick` method as shown in the following code snippet:

```
removeClick: function(){
    storage.removeUser(appGrid.getSelectedRowId());
},
```

Next, we need to reload the grid with the most up-to-date data from the `localStorage`.

callbacks.refreshGrid

The `refreshGrid` method updates the grid with the most recent data. Add the following code inside the `callbacks` object `refreshGrid` method as shown in the following code snippet:

```
refreshGrid: function(){
    appGrid.clearAll();
    appGrid.parse(storage.getUserGrid(), "json");
    callbacks.setToolbarItemStates();
},
```

When the `refreshGrid` method is used it first clears all data from the grid then retrieves the data from the `localStorage` to display in the grid.

After the grid is cleared and data is loaded the **remove** button is disabled.

callbacks.dataChanged

The data in the `localStorage` is changed whenever a user is added, edited, or removed. The `dataChanged` method will be used any time this happens to refresh any component that is using the data. Add the `refreshGrid` to the `callbacks` object `dataChanged`.

```
dataChanged: function(){
    callbacks.refreshGrid();
}
```

Now refresh the page. The following screenshot shows us what we should have after we refreshed:

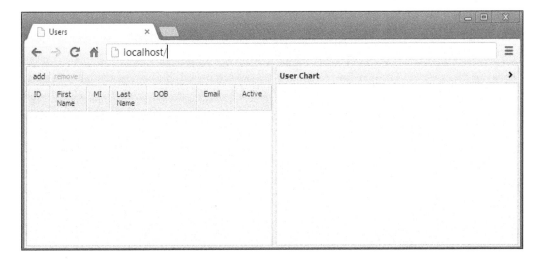

Testing the grid

Now, we are going to add a couple users with the `storage` methods to test the grid. After testing we will clear the `localStorage`.

Creating a user

The `createUser` method was created in *Chapter 3, Data Structures, Storage, and Callbacks* to add a user to the `localStorage`. We will use this to add two users to the grid and test the functionality. We will use a simplified version of the user object.

In the console type and run the following code snippet:

```
storage.createUser({firstName: "George", dob: new Date("1991")});
storage.createUser({firstName: "Steve", dob: new Date("1982")});
```

The `createUser` saved the users into the `localStorage` then called the `dataChanged` method, which refreshed the grid. Now we know that when a user is added the grid will update. The following screenshot shows the grid with the two added users:

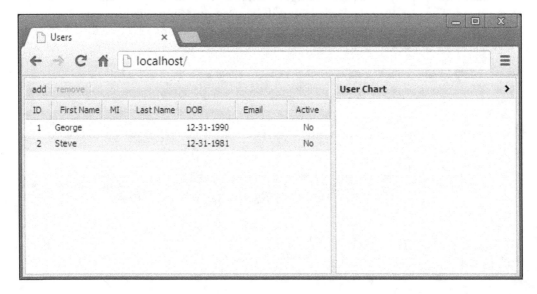

Removing a user

Now, we will test removing a user. Select a grid row and click on the **remove** button. The selected row is now removed. Clicking on the **remove** button removes the user from the localStorage and refreshes the grid.

Type and run the following code line in the console:

```
localStorage.clear();
```

Now refresh the page to clear the grid and reset the ID count.

Summary

In this chapter, we learned about the DHTMLX grid component. We also added the user grid to the application and tested it with the storage and callbacks methods.

In the next chapter, we will go over DHTMLX's Window component that will provide a pop-up to hold the form to edit and add a user.

7
The DHTMLX Window

In this chapter, we will learn about the DHTMLX window component covering the different initializations, events, methods, and settings. We will then add a pop-up window to the application that will hold a form created in the next chapter.

All changes done in this chapter will be inside the app.js file.

The DHTMLX window

The DHTMLX window component allows us to create multiple pop-up windows inside a web page quickly and easily. The window component provides the means to quickly attach a DTHMLX form, layout, grid, and most other components. It also does the work for styling, alignment, and positioning.

The DHTMLX window component is a base object that can have many child pop-up windows created from it. The base object takes all of the important settings like the image path and the optional viewport.

By the end of this chapter, we will have an excellent understanding of how to initialize and control a DHTMLX window object and create pop-up windows. We will then create a pop-up window that will open when the add button is pressed.

The methods and events

We will begin by creating a new instance of the base dhtmlXWindows object. Refresh the browser to clear any console code from previous exercises.

Initialization

Initializations of DHTMLX's components are either done through an existing component, such as the layout component, or initialized to a DOM element. This is different with the window component. The base object must be created first. From this base object, a set of new windows can be created.

The settings for initialization in the other discussed components have always been added in a functional manner. DHTMLX also provides the optional object literal way of applying settings to initialization for most of their components. For the first exercise we will create multiple windows with the settings as an object literal.

Creating the base object

In the console we will create a new dhtmlXWindows object with a settings object. This settings object will set the path to the images folder and allow the creation of multiple windows at the same time.

Type and run the following code in the console:

```
var myWindows = new dhtmlXWindows({
    image_path: config.imagePath,
    wins: [
        {
            id: "w1",
            height: 200,
            width: 200,
            text: "One"
        },
        {
            id: "w2",
            height: 200,
            width: 200,
            text: "Two",
            left: 20,
            top: 20
        },
        {
            id: "w3",
            height: 200,
            width: 200,
            text: "Three",
            left: 40,
            top: 40
        }
    ]
});
```

Three new pop-up windows were created in the page. Each of these pop-up windows can be moved around freely within the browser window similar to a desktop window.

Next we will create the windows through provided methods.

Create windows through methods

First we will create a new dhtmlXWindows method and then apply its settings.

Refresh the page. Type and run the following code in the console:

```
var myWindows = new dhtmlXWindows();
myWindows.setImagePath(config.imagePath);
```

Now we have a base object available to start the exercises that will create the individual pop-up windows.

Methods

Each individual pop-up window acts as a container. This means they can have other components attached to them. This is a nice feature. Using the pop-up window's methods, we can create and attach components like a form, grid, chart, layout, and more.

Now let's create a pop-up window.

createWindow (base object method)

The parameters for this method are ID, x position, y position, width, and height. Note that we will pass null for the position variables, as they are not required unless a screen position is desired.

Type and run the following code in the console:

```
var myPopup = myWindows.createWindow("w1", null, null, 200, 200);
```

We have just created a new pop-up window and assigned a reference to the myPopup variable. Using this, we will apply some of the available settings and methods.

setDimension

The setDimension sets the height and width of a pop-up window in pixels.

Type and run the following code in the console:

```
myPopup.setDimension(300,300);
```

denyResize

When a pop-up window is first created, the borders can be used to resize the window manually. The denyResize method disables this feature.

Type and run the following code in the console:

```
myPopup.denyResize();
```

This method also disables the maximize button on the pop-up window's toolbar. The allowResize method turns that feature back on.

centerOnScreen

The centerOnScreen method takes out any guess work of positioning a pop-up window. This method positions the pop-up window in the center of the page.

Type and run the following code in the console:

```
myPopup.centerOnScreen();
```

Now the pop-up window is centered.

setModal

The setModal method creates an overlay that covers the background application on the page. This is quite useful when restricting access to functionality other than the active pop-up window.

Type and run the following code in the console:

```
myPopup.setModal(true);
```

When the pop-up window is closed, the modal is also removed. But for the next, hide method, this does not occur. The modal remains even though the pop-up window is not visible.

hide

The hide method hides the pop-up window leaving its state the same as before it was hidden.

Type and run the following code in the console:

```
myPopup.hide();
```

The pop-up window is no longer on the screen, yet we still have the modal left over from our setModal method. Let's turn that off.

Type and run the following code in the console:

```
myPopup.setModal(false);
```

show

The `show` method does the opposite of our `hide` method. It shows the pop-up window once again.

Type and run the following code in the console:

```
myPopup.show();
```

It is visible again, right where we left it.

setText

The `setText` method allows us to change the title on the pop-up window.

Type and run the following code in the console:

```
myPopup.setText("My Popup Window!");
```

hideHeader

The `hideHeader` method allows us to hide the title bar all together.

Type and run the following code in the console:

```
myPopup.hideHeader();
```

showHeader

The `showHeader` method does the reverse of `hideHeader`.

Type and run the following code in the console:

```
myPopup.showHeader();
```

We touched on some of the basic methods for the pop-up window and all of the necessary ones for the application.

Events

With the DHTMLX window component, you can attach one event to all of the pop-up windows created from the same base object. This is achieved by attaching the event to the base object. You can also attach an event to each individual pop-up window.

We will be using the `onClose` event for the application. Let's do a quick exercise using this event.

onClose

The `onClose` event triggers just before the pop-up window closes. This allows us some freedom to manipulate something prior to it actually closing. It can also be used to prevent it from closing.

When the `onClose` event is attached to a pop-up window, we must return a `true` value from the handler we provide or it will not close.

Type and run the following code in the console:

```
myPopup.attachEvent("onClose",function(){
    console.log("close clicked");
});
```

Now try to close the pop-up window with the close button. The event is fired and the text is logged in the console but the popup does not close.

Type and run the following code in the console:

```
myPopup.detachAllEvents();
myPopup.attachEvent("onClose",function(){
    console.log("close clicked again");
    return true;
});
```

We detached the previously added event, then added a new event that returns true allowing the event to complete.

Next we will create the pop-up window for the application.

The application code

The application code for this chapter will create a pop-up window that will open when a grid row is double-clicked or when the when the **add** button on the toolbar is pressed. Once the pop-up window is created we do not want to recreate it again; so we will only hide and show it. To prevent the pop-up window from closing when the close button is pressed we will use the `onClose` event we discussed in the previous section.

Creating the pop-up window

Open the app.js file and add the following code at the end:

```
// Popup
var appPopup;
dhtmlxEvent(window, "load", function(){
    // create popup
    var win = new dhtmlXWindows();
    win.setImagePath(config.imagePath);
    appPopup = win.createWindow(1,null,null,400,300);
    appPopup.setText("User Add/Edit");
    appPopup.centerOnScreen();
    // popup events
    appPopup.attachEvent("onClose",callbacks.hidePopup);
    // hide popup initially
    appPopup.hide();
});
```

First we created the global variable as a reference to the pop-up window. Then we created the base object, attached an event, and lastly we made the popup hidden initially.

Next we will add the code to show and hide the pop-up window in the callbacks object.

callbacks

Inside the callbacks object we are editing the addClick, showPopup, and hidePopup methods to the following:

showPopup

The showPopup method contains the code to show the pop-up window and modal.

Add the code to the callbacks object's showPopup method as shown:

```
showPopup: function(){
    appPopup.setModal(1);
    appPopup.show();
},
```

hidePopup

The `hidePopup` method contains the code to hide the pop-up window and clear the modal.

Add the code to the `callbacks` object's `hidePopup` method as shown:

```
hidePopup: function(){
    appPopup.setModal(0);
    appPopup.hide();
}
```

addClick

The `addClick` method is triggered when the **add** button is pressed.

Add the code to the `callbacks` object's `addClick` method as shown:

```
addClick: function(){
    callbacks.showPopup();
}
```

Test our popup

All of the methods are now in place for the pop-up window.

To test we will first refresh the page. After refreshing there will be no noticeable difference until we click on the **add** button in the toolbar. Do so now and see that the pop-up window opens centered on the page with the modal covering the background application. Now test the close button and re-open.

With the pop-up window open, your application should look like the following screenshot:

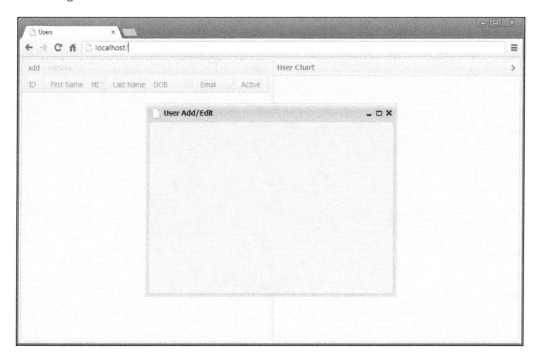

Summary

In this chapter, we learned about DHTMLX's window component, and the various ways through which we can initialize it. We also went over some of the important methods and events for the individual pop-up windows and how they relate to the base window object. Then we applied this knowledge to the application by adding the pop-up code and methods.

In the next chapter, we will use the pop-up window and add a DHTMLX form. This will allow us to add a user through the application as opposed to the console.

8
The DHTMLX Form and Calendar

In this chapter, we will learn about the DHTMLX form and calendar component covering the different initializations, methods, and settings. We will then add a form to the pop-up window that we created in the previous chapter.

All changes done in this chapter will occur inside the app.js and index.html files.

The DHTMLX form

The DHTMLX form component allows us to create HTML forms through code or convert existing HTML into a DHTMLX styled form. We will cover how to create a form through code using an array of JavaScript object literals.

The form component has many different item types. To name a few there are button, checkbox, container, input, file, hidden, label, multiselect, password, radio, select, template, textarea, and upload items. In addition there are also positional related items and items that integrate other components.

The DHTMLX calendar is one of those components that can be integrated into the form. It is still handled as an individual component once created. This means that its events and methods are handled separately.

By the end of this chapter, we will have a good understanding of the DHTMLX form and how to apply validation, populate the form and retrieve its data. We will then apply this understanding to the application and create a user add/edit form that will control the data entry and manipulation.

Initialization of the DHTMLX form

As we have covered in the previous chapters, when creating DHTMLX components we can either attach them to a DOM element or to a DHTMLX Layout. Same goes for the form component. So we do not need to cover these, instead, we will try something new which is similar to attaching a form to a layout.

In the last chapter, we learned how we can attach components directly to a pop-up window. This is how we will attach a form.

First, we will create an array of objects that contain the settings and form items. This will be used to initiate a form to the existing pop-up window. Here, we will practice by adding a form directly to the pop-up window with the `attachForm` method.

attachForm

The form we will create for the exercise will have the `settings`, `input`, `checkbox`, `calendar`, `select`, `button`, `block`, and `newcolumn` item. The form will not look that great but we are just going over what each item does.

Click on the **add** button to show our empty pop-up window then we will use the `attachForm` method to create a form in the pop-up window.

 When creating large blocks of code to place in the console, it helps to first type it into notepad or some simple text editor for ease of syntax and later editing.

In the console type in and run:

```
var myForm = appPopup.attachForm([
    {
        type: "settings",
        position: "label-left",
        labelWidth: 100
    },
    {
        type: "input",
        label: "No name:",
        inputWidth: 50
    },
    {
        type: "input",
```

```
            name: "input1",
            label: "Some Label:",
            required: true
        },
        {
            type: "checkbox",
            name: "checkbox1",
            label: "Yes?"
        },
        {
            type: "calendar",
            name: "mydate",
            label: "date:"
        },
        {
            type: "select",
            name: "mySelect",
            label: "Select One:",
            options: [
                { text: "Option1", value: 1 },
                { text: "Option2", value: 2 },
            ]
        },
        {
            type: "button",
            name: "myButton1",
            value: "Click Me"
        },
        {
            type: "block",
            list: [
                { type: "button", value: "Button Left"},
                { type: "newcolumn", offset: 55 },
                { type: "button", value: "Button Right"},
            ]
        }
    ]);
```

After you run this, you will see a form in the pop-up window that looks like the following screenshot:

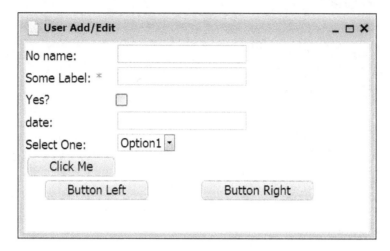

Let's go over each of these form item types and their attributes. Since we assigned a reference of the newly created form to the variable `myForm`, we will use this to call some methods.

Form items and attributes

Each item on the form has its own attributes that can be applied. Some are common across multiple item types. Here are some of the common attributes available that can be applied to most of the form items:

- `className` (string): It adds a CSS class to item
- `disabled` (Boolean): It disables or enables the item
- `hidden` (Boolean): It shows or hides the item
- `tooltip` (string): It sets a tooltip for the item
- `name` (string): It is the name of the `form` element

settings

The first object we have in the array is the settings item. This is an optional item that allows us to apply properties to all of the other items at once. For instance, having to set a width to all of the inputs in a form that has 20 inputs would be a little redundant. So, DHTMLX provided the settings object which works nicely. Don't worry the settings can be overridden at the individual item level.

For this exercise, we will also aligned the labels to the left using position and set a width to make them appear evenly using labelWidth.

input

The input type is a normal form input that you would see on any HTML form. The attributes we set on the inputs are inputWidth, validate, required, label, and name. The name is how we will later retrieve the value of this input in code.

Notice that there are three input items and one without the name attribute. If a name is not provided for a form item, DHTMLX generates a unique one for us. This does not make it easy to retrieve the values so we will use names in the application.

The validate attribute added to an input validates the value of that input on a specified rule. Some of the provided validation rules are ValidSSN, ValidNumeric, Empty, NotEmpty, and ValidEmail.

Another feature of the validate attribute is that a custom validation rule can be created. This is done by passing a custom function name or even a regular expression as the validate property value. Multiple validations can also be applied to the same item by using a string with the comma separating the validation, such as NotEmpty and ValidNumeric.

There is also the required property. This does the exact same as the NotEmpty validation, but also adds an asterisk next to the label automatically. The asterisk mark is common practice for web forms to notify the user that those fields are required.

We will test how these validations work shortly.

hidden

The hidden type is identical to the HTML input type of hidden. This allows us to place values on to a form that are not visible in the UI. We didn't use it in the exercise but we will be using this in the application form.

checkbox

The checkbox type creates an HTML checkbox with an integer value of 1 or 0. We can also add the required and validate attributes to a checkbox.

calendar

The calendar type creates an input and initializes the DHTMLX calendar component to it automatically. This form type has some additional properties over the normal form elements.

When creating a calendar, there is the option to format the date for display and set if we want time to be enabled using the dateFormat form item attribute. If you do not set the format it will be set to the default format.

The value retrieved from a form item that has a calendar component attached is a JavaScript date object. This is important to know when saving the value to a database or wanting to redisplay it later. We need to convert the JavaScript date object to a readable string for storage and retrieval.

select

The select type creates an HTML select with the property called options, which is an array that allows us to add HTML options to the select. We can also add the required and validate attributes to a select type. Inside each of the options objects, we can set the attribute selected to set an option as selected.

button

The button item type creates a form button. These buttons allows us to listen for the onButtonClick form event. The value property is what sets the text inside the button. We also added a couple more buttons that are inside the block item type.

block

DHTMLX provides several form items that assist with the form layout. The block form item is one of those. This creates a new group of form items that we can position together. The one we created contains the buttons and has several attributes, like the width attribute.

We added the form items to a block by using the list property, which is an array of form item objects no different than what we are using outside of the block item. Inside the list, we created the save and cancel buttons in different columns with the newcolumn item.

newcolumn

When the form item type newcolumn is added to a list of form items, it moves all of the items following the newcolumn item in the array to a new column. The only property available for this item is the offset, which sets the spacing between the columns.

As you can see, the last two buttons in the exercise form are in two different columns. If we have not placed them inside a block item before using the new column item, then it would have pushed the buttons to the right of the other form elements. The block item allowed us to contain the column without affecting the other form items.

Form methods

We just covered many of the DHTMLX form item types and some of their attributes. The DHTMLX form documentation has much more that was not covered.

Now, we will look into some of the methods for validation and manipulating the values in a form.

setItemFocus()

The setItemFocus method allows us to put focus on a form item of choice. This is pretty standard when creating forms and makes for a better user experience.

Type and run the following code line in the console:

```
myForm.setItemFocus("input1");
```

The cursor will be focused in the form item named input1 when the pop-up window is active.

validate()

The validate method runs the validation rules that were set on each form item.

Type and run the following code line in the console:

```
myForm.validate();
```

You will notice that the label for the required input is red and so will the text if any is entered. If there is no text in that field, enter some and leave it there. Now, run the validate method again. It will now check it once again and clears the validation on that input.

clear()

The `clear` method resets the values in the form. Enter some data in the input or select a date. Then, type and run the following code line in the console:

```
myForm.clear();
```

All the data is now removed. This will also clear any validation errors that may be present.

enableLiveValidation()

The `enableLiveValidation` runs the validate method on blur of the form item.

Type and run the following in the console:

```
myForm.enableLiveValidation(true);
```

Now, when you are focused on the required input and move to the next it will run the `validate` method. We can also turn this off by passing in `false`.

setFormData()

The `setFormData` method allows us to programmatically set the form item values. The parameter this method takes is a JavaScript object literal with the keys as the form item names and their values. This allows us to populate an entire form in one method if necessary. Let's add data to our form item named `input1`.

Type the following code line in the console and run:

```
myForm.setFormData({ input1: "Hello!" });
```

Now, the form item named `input1` has the entered value.

getFormData()

The `getFormData` method retrieves the values from the form, returning a JavaScript object literal.

Type the following code line in the console and run:

```
myForm.getFormData()
```

The returned object is logged in the console. Each of the form items are there. Notice the very first property is a random name generated by DHTMLX for the input that we did not provide a name for.

The application code

Now, we have covered all the necessary form methods to create the application form. We are now going to add the form creation method to the `app.js` that contains the form initialization, events, flags, and validations.

app.js

Open the `app.js` file and add the following code at the end:

```
// Form
var appForm;
dhtmlxEvent(window,"load", function(){
   // create form
   appForm = appPopup.attachForm([
     // settings
     {
        type: "settings", position: "label-left",
        labelWidth: 130, inputWidth: 120
     },
     // id
     {
        type: "hidden", name: "id"
     },
     // firstName
     {
        type: "input", name: "firstName",
        required: true, label: "First Name:"
     },
     // middleInitial
     {
        type: "input", name: "middleInitial",
        label: "Middle Initial:", inputWidth: 50
     },
     // lastName
     {
        type: "input", name: "lastName",
        required: true, label: "Last Name:"
     },
     // dob
     {
        type: "calendar", enableTime: false,
        dateFormat: "%n-%j-%Y", name: "dob",
        required: true, label: "Date of Birth:",
        inputWidth: 80
     },
     // email
     {
```

```
            type: "input", name: "email", required: true,
            validate: "ValidEmail", label: "Email:"
        },
        // active
        {
            type: "checkbox", name: "active",
            label: "Active:"
        },
        // buttons
        {
            type: "block",
            width: 300,
            list: [
                {
                    type: "button", value: "Save",
                    name: "save"
                },
                {
                    type: "newcolumn"
                },
                {
                    type: "button", value: "Cancel", name: "cancel"
                }
            ]
        }
]);

// enable validation
appForm.enableLiveValidation(true);

// set event
appForm.attachEvent("onButtonClick", function(btnName){
    // save or cancel
    if(btnName == "cancel"){
        callbacks.hidePopup();
    }else if(appForm.validate()){
        var formData = appForm.getFormData();
        if(formData.id){
            storage.updateUser(formData);
        }else{
            storage.createUser(formData);
        }
        callbacks.hidePopup();
    }
});
});
```

We first created the global variable `appForm` to reference the form we created. Then, inside the page load event handler we created the form and attached its events for the button clicks. We also added live validation and validation when clicked on the **save** button.

Inside the `onButtonClick` event handler is where we determine whether we are cancelling, editing, or adding a user. By checking if the hidden form field id has a value, we know whether to edit or add a new user. We then respectively use the `storage` object's `updateUser` or `createUser` method passing the entire form value object. Finally, the pop-up window is closed if there are no validation errors or if the **cancel** button was pressed.

callbacks

Inside the `callbacks` object, we will now add some code to the `editClick`, `showPopup`, and `hidePopup` methods.

showPopup()

In the `showPopup` method, we have already added the methods to show and set the pop-up modal. Now that we have a form created and we want to set focus on the first input field when the pop up opens.

Edit the `showPopup` method and add the following new code as shown:

```
showPopup: function(){
    appPopup.setModal(1);
    appPopup.show();
    appForm.setItemFocus("firstName");
},
```

hidePopup()

The `hidePopup` method already has the methods to hide the pop up. Now, when the pop up is hidden we want to clear the form values.

Edit the `hidePopup` method and add the following new code:

```
hidePopup: function(){
    appPopup.setModal(0);
    appPopup.hide();
    appForm.clear();
},
```

editClick()

The `editClick` is fired when we double-click on one of the user rows in the grid. In this chapter where we created the grid we attached the `onDblClick` event that passes the user id into the `callbacks` object `editClick` method. Now we will use this to retrieve the stored user information and populate the form.

We use the `storage` method `getUser` to retrieve the user object and the form method `setFormData` to populate those values into the form.

Edit the `editClick` method and add the following new code:

```
editClick: function(userId){
    // get user
    var user = storage.getUser(userId);
    // load user into popup
    appForm.setFormData(user);
    // show popup
    callbacks.showPopup();
},
```

This was the last change we needed to make in the `callbacks` object for the form. Next, we will add some CSS to the `index.html` to make it look a little better.

Edit the CSS form

Refresh the page and click on the **add** button to show the pop-up window and newly created form. As you will see in the following screenshot, the form contents are crowded along the edges of the pop-up window:

Let's fix this using CSS.

DHTMLX provides the option of editing the CSS to meet our needs, and we will do this now.

index.html

Open the `index.html` file and locate the internal CSS styles in the `head` tag. Edit the `style` tag as shown in the following code snippet:

```
body, html { height: 100%; width: 100%; }
.dhxform_base { margin: 25px; }
.dhxform_base .dhxform_base { margin: 20px 15px;}
```

We added styling to the CSS class `dhxform_base` and nested CSS class `dhxform_base`. DHTMLX adds this class to the outer container of the entire form and each column created inside of the form.

Now, refresh the page to see the newly applied styling. The pop-up window should now looks like the following screenshot:

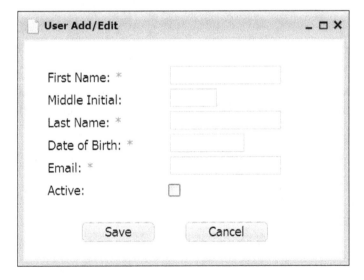

Test the application form

Now that the form is created and connected to the storage through the `callback` methods we can test. First, make sure the `localStorage` is cleared.

Type and run the following code line in the console:

```
localStorage.clear();
```

Now refresh the page.

Any users that were once in the grid should now be gone.

Go through your own testing of all the following actions:

- Add a user
- Double-click on a user in the grid and edit
- Select a user row in the grid and remove a user

All of these actions will refresh the grid as data is changed. You will also notice the validation on the required fields.

Summary

In this chapter, we covered the DHTMLX's form, which used a DHTMLX calendar implementation. We learned about initiating and attaching a form in a pop-up window and form validations. Then, we added the application code that allows us to add and edit users.

In the next chapter, we will learn about the DHTMLX chart component and create a bar chart that will automatically update each time any user data is changed.

9
The DHTMLX Chart

In this chapter, we will learn about the DHTMLX chart component and cover the different initializations, events, methods, and settings. We will then add a chart to the application.

All changes done in this chapter will occur inside the app.js and index.html files.

The DHTMLX chart component allows us to create many different types of charts with very little effort. DHTMLX provides chart types including area, horizontal bar, vertical bar, stacked vertical bar, stacked horizontal bar, donut, line, pie, radar, scatter, and spline. It is a very powerful collection of charts.

For the application we will be focusing on the vertical bar chart and learn how to structure data and use its events.

By the end of this chapter, we will have a great understanding of the chart component and add a bar chart to the application to display each user by their age.

The methods and events

We will begin by initializing a chart, adding data, defining a series, and manipulating the chart settings. After we have created a chart to test with we will attach one of the available events.

Initialization of the DHTMLX chart

Same as the other the DHTMLX components we covered, a chart can be attached to a DOM element or a DHTMLX layout cell.

One important thing to know during initialization is that the chart requires a JavaScript object literal as an argument or an exception will occur. This JavaScript object can contain the settings and series for the chart or be left empty, allowing the settings and series to be added later.

dhtmlXChart()

The DOM initialization approach is achieved by creating a new `dhtmlXChart` object and setting the JavaScript object argument `container` property value to the DOM element's ID. This would look like the following code. Do not enter this in the console:

```
var myChart = new dhtmlXChart({ container: "myContainerId" });
```

addChart()

The `addChart` method is actually part of the DHTMLX layout cell object and attaches a chart directly to the cell of our choosing. Now, we will attach a chart to the `appLayout` cell `b`.

Type and run the following code line in the console:

```
var myChart = appLayout.cells("b").attachChart({});
```

Here, we initialized a chart to a cell and assigned a reference to as the `myChart` variable. We will use this chart for the following exercises.

Methods

Now we will begin the exercises for the chart methods.

refresh()

The `refresh` method allows newly applied settings to show in the chart. If a chart setting is changed or added the `refresh` method must be used or those settings will not go into effect.

It is implemented by the following code:

```
myChart.refresh();
```

add()

The `add` method allows us to add data to a chart. Think of these as rows coming from a database or local storage. This method takes a JavaScript object literal as an argument. Each of the objects added to the chart must have properties of the same name to compare or display.

Let us pretend that we have a social profile site with several persons. We know their name, age, and number of views their profile has. We will use this to add some data to the chart for viewing.

Type and run the following code in the console:

```
myChart.add({ name: "Steve", age: 45, profileViews: 83 });
myChart.add({ name: "John", age: 27, profileViews: 115 });
myChart.add({ name: "Ashley", age: 34, profileViews: 225 });
```

Data is refreshed automatically to the chart. As soon as this data is added we will see a circle like the following screenshot:

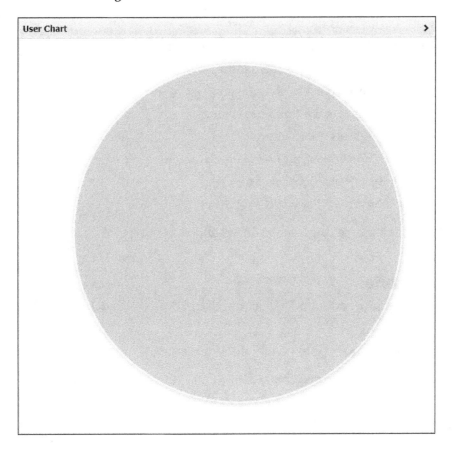

We are seeing this grey circle because DHTMLX chart defaults as a pie chart and we did not apply any settings to the chart to tell it which data to use for comparison.

Next we will define those settings.

define()

The define method allows us to individually change the chart's settings and first data series. It takes two parameters. The first being the name of the property we will set and the second value of that property, which could be a string, object, Boolean, or integer depending on the property.

Here are some of the settings:

- view: (string) sets the type of chart
- container: (string) used in DOM initialization
- padding: (object, int) sets the padding of the chart
- legend: (object) creates a chart legend
- value: (string) sets the first series value
- label: (string) sets the first series label
- gradient: (function, string) sets value gradient
- x axis: (object) sets the x axis properties
- y axis: (object) sets the y axis properties

Please note that these settings can be different per chart type. We are building a bar chart.

Define a series

First we will define a series that will let the chart know which data we want to compare.

The series is broken down into several different settings:

- value (the value to be compared)
- label (the label for each value)
- color (the color for that series)

When applying the value and label to the chart they use a template syntax, which allows for the combining of properties from the compared objects. Each property must have the # as a prefix and suffix.

Now, we will add a new series by adding the value setting. Remember, we need to refresh the chart after each setting is added.

Type and run the following code in the console:

```
myChart.define("value", "#profileViews#");
myChart.refresh();
```

This series we added is comparing the profile views that each of our data object received on our pretend social site.

Adding the value allowed us to see some colored slices, but we still don't know who they belong to. We will fix this with the label setting.

Type and run the following code in the console:

```
myChart.define("label", "#name#(#profileViews#)");
myChart.refresh();
```

We used the template syntax to show the name and profileViews in the label component. Now we know who each data set belongs to.

There is one issue, though with the display of the chart. Resize your browser window until the labels are only partially visible. This can be fixed by defining padding to the chart.

Type and run the following code in the console:

```
myChart.define("padding",100);
myChart.refresh();
```

This will give the chart a padding of 100 pixels inside the layout cell and now the labels have plenty of room to be readable. The chart now looks like the following screenshot:

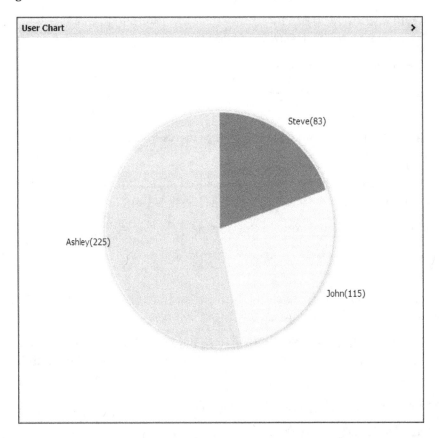

Define chart type

Now we will change the chart to a bar chart. We have already set the chart up with the first series of data. Let's see what happens when we change it to a bar chart with the `view` setting.

Type and run the following code in the console:

```
myChart.define("view","bar");
myChart.refresh();
```

Our chart has been changed to a bar chart. But the layout and labels don't look quite right. For this, we need to set the `xAxis` to show the labels at the bottom and change up some of the other settings. Let's do that now.

Type and run the following code in the console:

```
myChart.define("label", false);
myChart.define("padding", 50);
myChart.define("xAxis", {
    title: "Names",
    template: "#name#",
    lines: false
})
myChart.define("tooltip","Views (#profileViews#)");
myChart.refresh();
```

The chart is now more readable. We removed the label and added a tooltip which will display the number of profile views when the mouse is hovered over a bar in the chart.

The xAxis setting provides the ability to label the bottom of the chart with meaningful labels. As you can see, we added the title of Names and each data set has a label with the respective person's name. We also set the lines property to false, which removes the vertical lines from the chart.

The chart now looks like the following screenshot:

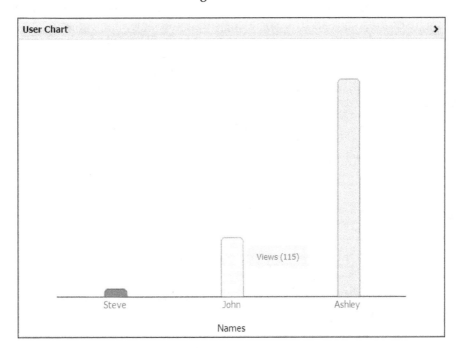

Next we will cover adding a second series of data to the chart.

addSeries()

The addSeries method allows us to create additional series for the chart. We must provide an object as an argument. Now we will add a data series for the age of each person in the chart.

Type and run the following code in the console:

```
myChart.addSeries({
    value: "#age#",
    color: "purple",
    tooltip: "Age (#age#)"
});
myChart.refresh();
```

Inside the object, we set the value, color, and tooltip then refreshed. This applied the changes and now the age series has been added.

idByIndex()

Each data object we added to the chart earlier has an index assigned from the chart's internal array. Meaning the first data object for Steve has the index of zero. Each of these data objects also has an ID associated with it and can be retrieved by using the idByIndex method. This will allow us to access the data object after it has been added.

Let's get the ID for the data object of Steve. Type and run the following code in the console:

```
var steveDataId = myChart.idByIndex(0);
```

Now, we have assigned the ID that was generated by DHTMLX to our steveDataId variable.

get()

The get method pulls all the data we added earlier with the add method for Steve. It takes the argument of the associated data ID we want to retrieve. The returned data object is not read-only. We can use that same object to change the values and refresh the grid to apply the changes.

Type and run the following code in the console:

```
var steveData = myChart.get(steveDataId);
```

You can see in the console that we have all the data that was originally created for Steve. Well, it appears Steve doesn't like to be called Steve but would rather be called Steven. Let's update that for him.

Type and run the following code in the console:

```
steveData.name  = "Steven";
myChart.refresh();
```

As you see his name is now changed.

Now we will look at the events.

Events

There are many events available for the chart. For now let's take a look at one of them to give us enough of an idea for future usage of the others available.

onItemClick

The `onItemClick` event is triggered when we click on each of the bars in our chart. It will return the data object ID of the clicked item. Let's use this event to show an alert telling us whose data we just clicked on.

Type and run the following code in the console:

```
myChart.attachEvent("onItemClick", function(id){
    alert("This is data for "+myChart.get(id).name);
});
```

Now, when we click each of the bars we see an alert telling us the name of that data.

We covered more than all of the necessary chart methods and events that are needed for the application. Let's start applying what we've learned.

The application code

For the application, we are going to show a series of data based on the age of each of our users added through the form. This will match up with the grid any time data is changed. As mentioned before we will be using a bar chart and will create all necessary settings in the initialization method with the passed in object.

First, we will add the creation method in our `app.js` file directly after our form creation method. This will have our global chart variable and create method.

Creating the chart

Add the following code to the app.js file at the end:

```
// Chart
var appChart;
dhtmlxEvent(window,"load",function(){
    appChart = appLayout.cells("b").attachChart({
        view: "bar",
        value: "#age#",
        label: "#age#",
        gradient: "rising",
        tooltip: {
            template: "#age#"
        },
        xAxis: {
            title: "Users",
            template: "#name#",
            lines: false
        },
        yAxis: {
            title: "Years of Age",
            lines: true
        },
        padding: {
            left: 25,
            right: 10,
            top: 45
        }
    });
    // reset chart data
    callbacks.refreshChart();
});
```

First, we created a global variable and then created a chart inside the page load event handler. Inside the chart initialization, we applied all the settings that we just learned with the addition of gradient and yAxis. The gradient sets a nice gradient effect on the bars. The yAxis will show lines and numbers for the ages on the left side of the chart.

After the initialization, we called the callbacks.refreshChart, which will refresh the chart data the same way we did for the grid.

callbacks.refreshChart()

Inside the `callbacks` object `refreshChart` method, we will clear and add data to the chart.

Edit the `refreshChart` method as shown in the following code:

```
refreshChart: function(){
    appChart.clearAll();
    appChart.parse(storage.getUserBarChart(),"json");
},
```

callbacks.dataChanged()

Inside the `callbacks` object `dateChanged` method, we will add the `refreshChart` method.

Edit the `dataChanged` method as follows:

```
dataChanged: function(){
    callbacks.refreshGrid();
    callbacks.refreshChart();
}
```

Now we can test the chart!

Test the application

First, clear our local storage data once again.

Type and run the following code in the console:

```
localStorage.clear()
```

Now, refresh the page and the chart and grid should be empty.

We are going to add some users to the application, but first we need to take a look at something. Click on the **add** button for the pop up. Move the pop-up window over the chart by dragging the header. In the current version, at the time of writing this book, the chart has a higher z-index than the pop-up window, which doesn't allow us to use the pop up correctly. This can be fixed with a small CSS change.

If you are having this issue, let's fix it by going into our `index.html` CSS and adding the following CSS to the end of our styles:

```
.dhx_chart{ z-index: 1; }
```

Now, refresh the page and try using the pop up once again. Everything works and the pop-up window is on top once again.

Let's start adding some data. Use the pop-up window to add the following users:

- John Smith, jsmith@email.com, 1-1-1963
- Tim Smith, tsmith@email.com, 1-1-1963
- Alice Chance, achance@email.com, 6-23-1972
- Bob White, bwhite@email.com, 12-22-1993
- Jimbo Manning, jmanning@email.com, 4-18-1984
- Peter Redding, predding@email.com, 9-9-2001
- Susie Cue, scue@email.com, 10-3-1989

As you were entering these users all data components were refreshing at the same time! Remember, we can always edit a user by double-clicking the grid row.

The chart is completed and looks like the following screenshot:

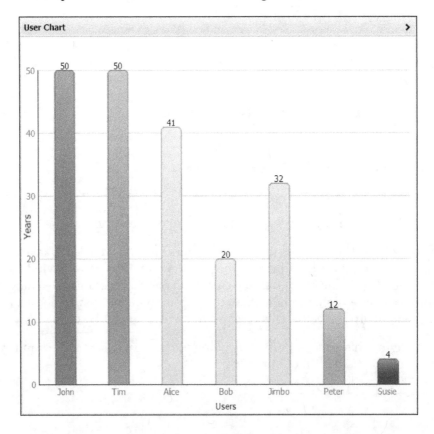

Summary

In this chapter, we discussed how to create a DHTMLX chart and manipulate it once created. With this newly learned skill, we were able to create a nice looking bar chart for the application.

In the next chapter, we will go over testing the application, troubleshooting and give ideas on how to expand it on your own.

10
The Finish Line

Welcome to the finish line! The application is now complete. With these newly perfected skills, we are ready to set forth into the world and use DHTMLX components on everything! Ok, that statement may have been a little overboard, but we do have a greater understanding of the library and should feel extremely comfortable in applying it.

In this chapter, we will go over some of the issues we may have experienced in the creation of the application. We will also talk about some additional things we could do to expand on it.

We will not be making any mandatory code changes in this chapter. But it is highly encouraged that you attempt some of the suggested additions on your own to further advance your skills.

Testing

In the previous chapter, we added a list of users and lightly tested the application. Now that it is all completed, it looks like the following screenshot:

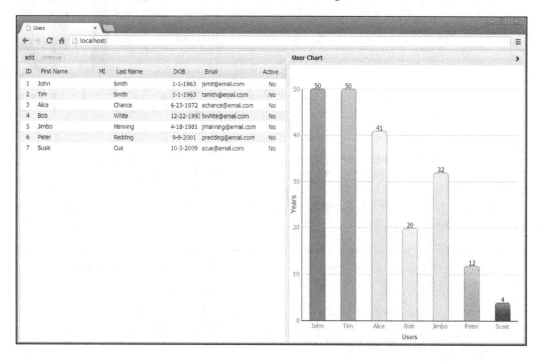

This is the time to test all of the functionality that was created. When testing, make sure you go through all of the points listed as follows:

- The form should have all of the correct validations
- The toolbar should enable and disable buttons and trigger the popup
- Double-clicking a row should open the form with user information
- Updating or adding a user should change the data in the grid and chart
- There should not be any z-index issues with the popup over the chart

Next let's talk about troubleshooting.

Troubleshooting

When developing in JavaScript, syntax errors are extremely common, because errors happen at runtime and editors for JavaScript can be extremely limited. But if you pay close attention to your developer console in Chrome it will take you straight to the error and give a pretty reasonable explanation with the provided exception.

Some of the most frequent things that happen are:

- Missing a trailing comma between items in an object
- Missing a parenthesis or bracket when using event handlers
- Case sensitivity in variables and methods

They may sound like simple issues and they are. If you are a seasoned developer, you already know those nuances. If not, always keep these in mind because it can save you a lot of time debugging to check those first. These types of syntax errors tend to happen after long hours in front of code.

The grid component can provide issues when first learning, particularly, the initialization. This is because the grid has a separate `init` method that is called after it is created and all of the settings are applied. So keep this in mind as well.

Next, let's talk about how to take the application to the next level.

More features

The application we built was a fairly simple application to get us familiar with the components. But, if we want to use this in a real world environment, it would need some tweaking.

Server side

HTML5's localStorage is excellent for storing data on the client side and even allowing web applications to work offline. But once this data needs to be shared among other web users there needs to be some type of server-side storage for each client to share changes to the data.

There are so many options to choose from. Personally, I would create a web service that would write to a server-side database. Because we separated all of our data calls into the `storage` object, essentially a **DAL** (**Data Access Layer**), all that we would need to do is adjust these methods and add some Ajax calls. The rest of the application would remain untouched. Well, except for adding some `progressOn` and `progressOff` methods.

Adding icons

Something we didn't go over in the earlier chapters is the additional icons. This is a really nice feature to add to any application.

Adding a plus image to the **add** button and a red x image to the **remove** button in the toolbar would make it look more professional. You can also use icons without text to save on toolbar space, and the tooltip feature to provide more information on the functionality of that button.

The default skin that we used in our application uses 18 X 18 pixel images, preferably a .png with a transparent background.

The pop-up window could also have an icon in the header. This could be set as a small user icon and perhaps change the icon depending on if we are adding or editing a user.

Check out each of the component's documentation for their methods on adding images and icons.

Event tweaks

One of the particular event tweaks that should be touched on is the event for the calendar in the form. If the date input is focused on, we could automatically trigger the calendar and not allow free entering of a date by the keyboard. But, this is by taste and not totally necessary since there is date validation. This one you can decide on.

One thing that I prefer to do is to apply the date value from the calendar when the year is selected. As of right now, to change the year for the dob of a user, you would need to select the year and day again before the calendar will apply the data change in the form. This can be quite annoying and can be fixed.

The calendar has an onChange event that triggers any time the value is changed in the calendar component. This event returns the value of the current calendar selected value. Using this event, you could update the value to the input any time the date is changed, whether it is the month, day, or year.

Here is what the code looks like to apply it to the application:

```
var dobCal = appForm.getCalendar("dob");
dobCal.attachEvent("onChange", function(date){
    appForm.setItemValue("dob", date);
});
```

This would go after the form initialization method and would work if you added it now.

Chart ideas

Another nice addition would be to allow the person using the application to change the chart type. There are several different approaches on how this could be accomplished. One of them would be to add a toolbar to the cell that has the chart in it. This toolbar could have a select button with the different chart types as options. When the select button changes, you could change the chart settings to match the selected chart type. You could also add icons next to each of the item's text or just have an icon for the option.

If you really wanted to get fancy, you could leave the chart empty with no data. Create an additional button on the toolbar to add users to the chart by choice. Therefore, when a user is selected in the grid and the newly created button is pressed, it would add the selected user's data to the chart. This would take some tweaking of the current code that retrieves the data. You may also want to create a clear button on the chart side to empty the data.

We could keep going for another 10 pages of where to take this application, but that wouldn't be creative on your part! So, now it's your turn! Give some thought to how this could grow and keep it in your toolbox of code for later referencing as you get better with the DHTMLX library!

Summary

In this chapter, we went over the application and some things to be vigilant of while developing in JavaScript and with the DHTMLX library. We also discussed some cool code additions and looked at a small sample for you to add on your own. This concludes programming of the user application with the DHTMLX library. I hope you take some of these mentioned ideas and mix them with your own to further develop the application.

Index

About Packt Publishing

Packt, pronounced "packed", published its first book *"Mastering phpMyAdmin for Effective MySQL Management"* in April 2004 and subsequently continued to specialize in publishing highly focused books on specific technologies and solutions.

Our books and publications share the experiences of your fellow IT professionals in adapting and customizing today's systems, applications, and frameworks. Our solution based books give you the knowledge and power to customize the software and technologies you're using to get the job done. Packt books are more specific and less general than the IT books you have seen in the past. Our unique business model allows us to bring you more focused information, giving you more of what you need to know, and less of what you don't.

Packt is a modern, yet unique publishing company, which focuses on producing quality, cutting-edge books for communities of developers, administrators, and newbies alike. For more information, please visit our website: www.packtpub.com.

Writing for Packt

We welcome all inquiries from people who are interested in authoring. Book proposals should be sent to author@packtpub.com. If your book idea is still at an early stage and you would like to discuss it first before writing a formal book proposal, contact us; one of our commissioning editors will get in touch with you.

We're not just looking for published authors; if you have strong technical skills but no writing experience, our experienced editors can help you develop a writing career, or simply get some additional reward for your expertise.

jQuery 1.4 Reference Guide

ISBN: 978-1-84951-004-2   Paperback: 336 pages

A comprehensive exploration of the popular
JavaScript library

1. Quickly look up features of the jQuery library

2. Step through each function, method, and
   selector expression in the jQuery library
   with an easy-to-follow approach

3. Understand the anatomy of a jQuery script

4. Write your own plug-ins using jQuery's
   powerful plug-in architecture

jQuery UI 1.8: The User Interface Library for jQuery

ISBN: 978-1-84951-652-5   Paperback: 424 pages

Build highly interactive web applications with
ready-to-use widgets from the jQuery User
Interface Library

1. Packed with examples and clear explanations
   of how to easily design elegant and powerful
   front-end interfaces for your web applications

2. A section covering the widget factory including
   an in-depth example on how to build a custom
   jQuery UI widget

3. Updated code with significant changes and
   fixes to the previous edition

Please check **www.PacktPub.com** for information on our titles

Responsive Web Design with HTML5 and CSS3

ISBN: 978-1-84969-318-9   Paperback: 324 pages

Learn responsive design using HTML5 and CSS3 to adapt websites to any browser or screen size

1. Everything needed to code websites in HTML5 and CSS3 that are responsive to every device or screen size

2. Learn the main new features of HTML5 and use CSS3's stunning new capabilities including animations, transitions and transformations

3. Real world examples show how to progressively enhance a responsive design while providing fall backs for older browsers

HTML5 Canvas Cookbook

ISBN: 978-1-84969-136-9   Paperback: 348 pages

Over 80 recipes to revolutionize the web experience with HTML5 Canvas

1. The quickest way to get up to speed with HTML5 Canvas application and game development

2. Create stunning 3D visualizations and games without Flash

3. Written in a modern, unobtrusive, and objected oriented JavaScript style so that the code can be reused in your own applications

Please check **www.PacktPub.com** for information on our titles